# Praise for *Speaker Camp*

*As an accomplished speaker who now teaches and encourages others in the field to speak publicly, this is the book I would have written. It's your A-to-Z guide for how to become a public speaker, covering every nook and cranny of the process. While it's tailored to those who work in the tech and design fields, anyone looking to become a public speaker can benefit from this book.*

**Jessica Ivins,**
**Senior UX Designer**

*The fear of public speaking sits amongst the highest possible fears, and understandably so. It's not easy to step in front of an audience, large or small, and present on a given topic. Fortunately,* Speaker Camp, *by Russ Unger and Samantha Starmer, will help you overcome that fear and prepare you to give the presentation you dream of. Working step by step from idea to creation to stepping on stage,* Speaker Camp *puts you in a position to give the perfect presentation. It's an enjoyable book filled with excellent insights and advice, well worth the read for new speakers or experienced veterans!*

**Shay Howe,**
**Designer, Front-End Developer, Problem Solver**

*This book provides a thorough walk-through of everything you need to think about and do as you grow to success as a conference speaker. The chapters each serve to coach, mentor, encourage, and caution the reader. If you're eager to increase your confidence in all aspects of conference speaking, then you definitely need this book.*

**Steve Portigal,**
**Author of *Interviewing Users: How to Uncover Compelling Insights***

*This is the book I wish I'd had when I first began applying to speak at conferences.* Speaker Camp *demystifies the process, answers the questions you'd be embarrassed to ask, and holds your hand as you create a proposal, build a presentation, and give the talk. It's going to make my next presentation a lot easier.*

**Laura Creekmore,**
**President of Creek Content**

# Praise for *Speaker Camp*

*Russ and Samantha know all there is to know about great conferences, as both are experienced speakers and savvy organizers. Let this book guide you through the entire process, and learn how to inspire your audience.*

**Cennydd Bowles,**
**Design Lead at Twitter, Author of *Undercover User Experience Design***

*Speaking at conferences is a common goal for designers, or anyone, really, who has become so interested in a topic that they want to share what they've seen and learned. But the steps to actually getting there—pulling together ideas, writing proposals, and pitching your presentation to organizers—can be daunting. It's hard to argue with Russ and Samantha's success in this space, and this book breaks down their thoughts and process in clear and intriguing ways. As an experienced speaker, reading it gave me new clarity and perspectives on the somewhat haphazard way I sometimes go about coming up with ideas for presentations and pitching them. I'll most certainly be recommending this to anyone who asks me for advice on getting into public speaking.*

**Adam Connor,**
**Design Director, Illustrator, Speaker**

*It is easy to go straight to designing the content and visual aids for a presentation, but they won't be seen if the proposal isn't given due time and won't be remembered if the presentation isn't well rehearsed and delivered. Speaker Camp gives clear tips and suggestions for every step in the speaking process, right down to investing in the right presentation tools. It is a must-read for anyone interested in speaking at conferences, workshops, or any event.*

**Tonia M. Bartz,**
**UX Designer, Ethnographer**

Speaker Camp *provides an incredibly methodical, but straightforward, guide for proposing and preparing presentations. Each section offers relevant questions to help you think through the nitty-gritty details that can often make or break your talk. It doesn't just cover slides and speaking technique; it helps you tailor your big idea to the audience and theme of the conference—thus making your talks more effective and, as a result, you more confident.*

**Amanda Morrow,**
**Interactive Designer at BitMethod**

# Praise for *Speaker Camp*

*There's no magical potion that makes public speaking any less terrifying, but with this book, Russ and Samantha have created the next best thing: a comprehensive, thoughtful, sensible approach to presenting and speaking. Though I have considerable client-facing presentation experience, I have spoken at only a few conferences and public venues, and* Speaker Camp *has helped demystify and de-terrify the conference preparation process for me.*

**Gabby Hon,**
**Senior User Experience Consultant**

*Setting yourself up to deliver a great presentation takes some serious prep work, and nobody knows it better than Starmer and Unger. In* Speaker Camp, *they've broken it down to a science. This playbook should be in the hands of everyone daring enough to take the stage and anyone hell-bent on nailing their next talk.*

**Dennis Kardys,**
**Design Director at WSOL, Author, Speaker**

*There are shelves of books about public speaking in the world. But this one, the one in your hands, is better. As a conference speaker and organizer, I can say this is the best practical guide I've read for creating an effective presentation, marketing yourself to conference organizers, and building the confidence to impress an audience. If only I'd had it when I began speaking...*

**J Cornelius,**
**Founder of Nine Labs, President of the Atlanta Web Design Group,**
**Creator of the Web Afternoon conference series**

*Smart, inspirational, and relentlessly practical,* Speaker Camp *weaves an insightful starter toolkit for preparing, submitting, and delivering impactful conference presentations. Its engaging style features carefully researched content supplemented by candid real-life examples, demystifying the ingredients of a great talk as seen through the eyes of seasoned speakers and content curators worldwide. A must-read for first-time presenters and useful reference material for those looking to fine-tune their craft.*

**Cornelius Rachieru,**
**Co-chair, UXcamp Ottawa**

# SPEAKER CAMP

**A SELF-PACED WORKSHOP FOR PLANNING, PITCHING, PREPARING, AND PRESENTING AT CONFERENCES**

RUSS UNGER

SAMANTHA STARMER

Foreword by **Jared Spool**

Speaker Camp: A Self-paced Workshop for Planning, Pitching, Preparing, and Presenting at Conferences
Russ Unger and Samantha Starmer

**New Riders**
www.newriders.com

To report errors, please send a note to errata@peachpit.com

New Riders is an imprint of Peachpit, a division of Pearson Education.

**Project Editor:** Michael J. Nolan
**Development Editor:** Jennifer Lynn/Page One Editing
**Production Editor:** Danielle Foster
**Copyeditor:** Jennifer Needham
**Indexer:** Joy Dean Lee
**Proofreaders:** Patricia Pane, Marta Justak
**Cover Designer:** Brad Simpson
**Interior Designer and Compositor:** Danielle Foster

ISBN 13: 978-0-321-96112-9
ISBN 10: 0-321-96112-9

9 8 7 6 5 4 3 2 1

Printed and bound in the United States of America

# Acknowledgments

## Mutual Gratitude

Jared Spool sat in on our first Speaker Camp workshop in Chicago and provided thoughtful critique and insight throughout the day, while also offering his guidance to the attendees during their individual presentations. On top of that, he has been generous with his time and advice, and we're flattered that he provided us with the Foreword to this book.

Dan Willis, that crazy genius, started off the Cranky Talk Workshops and invited both of us to be faculty. It was an amazing experience—one that changed our lives and made us dramatically better at this speaking at conferences stuff. We can't thank Dan enough for the opportunity, and we hope we've done this spin-off some justice. Our other Cranky Talk alums, Adam Polansky, Dan M. Brown, Karen McGrane, and Tom Willis, have all been a great source of inspiration, and we're deeply honored to have had the opportunity to work with and learn from each of you.

We are forever grateful to the many brilliant people who helped us through the writing of this book. We're thankful to have been able to get time with some of the brightest minds that we know, who shared their insights with us. In no particular order: Jeffrey Zeldman, Hugh Forrest, Barak Danin, Bruno Figueiredo, Clark Sell, Jen and Jim Remsik, Andy Budd, J Cornelius, Cornelius Rachieru, Brad Smith, Eric Reiss, Jonathon Colman, Adam Connor, Aaron Irizarry, Gabby Hon, Brad Nunnally, Kristina Halvorson, Dan M. Brown, Karen McGrane, Christian Lane, Eytan Mirsky, Jesse James Garrett, Susan Weinschenk, Jessica Ivins, Stephen P. Anderson, Shay Howe, Steve Portigal, Laura Creekmore, Cennydd Bowles, Nick Finck, Jess McMullin, Tonia M. Bartz, Amanda Morrow, Dennis Kardys, Christopher Mayfield, Andy Crestodina, Andy Hullinger, Gretchen Frickx, Dennis Schleicher, Tim Frick, Christian Crumlish, Drew McLellan, Bryan Eisenberg, Greg Nudelman, Carole Burns, and Brad Simpson.

We'd also like to thank everyone at New Riders who helped make this book possible: Michael Nolan, Glenn Bisignani, the Jens—Jennifer Lynn and Jennifer Needham—(who are amazing!), Aren Straiger, Danielle Foster, Patricia Pane, and Joy Dean Lee.

## Russ Unger

As usual, my wife, Nicolle, and our daughters, Sydney and Avery, taught me a lot about what it means to be supportive, if not hilarious, during a book-writing endeavor. I'm blessed to have a wonderful mother, a caring extended family, and a bunch of pretty incredible friends who offered their support and kindness along the way, too.

Samantha Starmer has been an outstanding partner through our workshop and book-writing enterprise—and I think we've had fun doing this juggling act with full-time jobs, life, and other crazy commitments!

Michael Nolan was really foundational in making this happen—he's got a long list of authors you know and love to read in his stable, and when we were talking about things happening in the world, it was his idea to turn Speaker Camp into a book. It's been a lot of fun to bring it to life, and I'm indebted to Michael for nudging (kicking) it in the right direction.

I had a lot of amazing friends and experts sharing their insight this time around, and they really helped to sand off some of the corners of the content. These folks are phenomenal, and if you ever have the opportunity to see one of them speak, attend one of their events, or meet them in person, you simply must make the effort to do so!

As always, the amazing Brad Simpson (www.i-rradiate.com) was the chief of helping out with all things of a visual design nature for the home team. I had great support from Gabby Hon, Brad Nunnally, Laura Creekmore, Whitney Hess, Karl Fast, Jesse James Garrett, David Armano, Christian Lane, Eytan Mirsky, Alex Dittmer, Jeffrey Zeldman, Hugh Forrest, Barak Danin, Bruno Figueiredo, Clark Sell, Jen and Jim Remsik, Andy Budd, J Cornelius, Brad Smith, Eric Reiss, Ric Soens, Chris Fahey, Adam Connor, Aaron Irizarry, Kristina Halvorson, Dan M. Brown, Karen McGrane, Susan Weinschenk, Jessica Ivins, Stephen P. Anderson, Shay Howe, Steve Portigal, Cennydd Bowles, Tonia M. Bartz, Amanda Morrow, Dennis Kardys, Christian Crumlish, Drew McLellan, Bryan Eisenberg, Greg Nudelman, Carole Burns, the late Dr. Arthur Doederlein, the Chicago Build Guild, the Cranky Talkers, Lou Rosenfeld and all of the Rosenfeld Media Experts, the Chicago Camps (http://chicagocamps.org) team, all the people who attended and helped out with our first Speaker Camp workshop, and everyone else who may have been inadvertently overlooked—you were all very much a part of helping to make this happen. And Jonathan "Yoni" Knoll.

## Samantha Starmer

When Russ Unger first raised the idea of *Speaker Camp*, I couldn't decide if I was thrilled or terrified. I decided that both emotions meant I just had to take the plunge and thus undertook this fantastic journey. Russ has been an incredible partner and friend, and everything great about this effort comes down to his amazing energy and his abilities to herd cats with grace and to always make me smile. I would willingly walk any future tightrope with Russ leading the way.

There are so many people over the years who have inspired me, taught me, and mentored me to become a better speaker and to always continue learning. In order not to miss any of them inadvertently, I'm not going to attempt a comprehensive list. But I have a vivid memory of James Robertson convincing me many years ago while at an early IA Summit that I, too, might have something to say. Thanks to James for that not-so-subtle nudge that helped start all of this wonderful craziness. And thanks to every student I've taught, employee I've worked with, and person I've mentored and been mentored by. Each and every one of you has given me courage and made your mark.

And the biggest thanks to my husband, Sean, who has supported me in everything I want to do, even when it means that he is always the one to cook dinner and clean the cat box.

# Contents

# Foreword

I go to a lot of conferences every year—probably 40 to 50 of them. At many of them, I give a presentation. But that's not the real reason I go.

The real reason I go is because I'm looking to hear new presenters. I want to hear their thinking. I'm really interested in the twist they'll put on a method or concept. I'm thrilled when I can hear about the journey they've taken.

Most of these folks are presenting for the first time. They've never been in front of any audience, and now they're in front of their peers, sharing these new ideas. And that's exciting.

What's even more exciting is finding someone who is really good. Their story is solid. Their presentation techniques are polished. I'm sucked right into what they're saying, and they've got me hooked.

It's like discovering a new band nobody has ever heard of or eating at a new restaurant that the crowds haven't found yet. There I am, in the room, hearing this great talk.

Here's the funny thing: The odds are *against* this happening. The first-time presentation business is a really tough one to succeed in.

When I was younger—much younger—I did a lot of acting. When I first started, I was handed a script to perform from. Not just any script, but a vetted, popular script. (It was a Neil Simon play. I played a grumpy cop with a couple of dozen lines. Funny stuff, if I said it right.)

I also had a great director. She had wonderful patience with me as a new actor. She gave me solid direction, often multiple times, until I finally "got it." We rehearsed my part for weeks before the first performance, and I was able to really hone my performance.

All the advantages I had as a first-time actor are not what we give our first-time presenters. We ask them to write their own scripts instead of using vetted ones. We insist they do all their own direction instead of working under the guidance of someone experienced. Most of these presentations should, just by the nature of how they happen, be miserable performances by obvious amateurs.

Yet I go to these conferences, plunk myself in the session room, and voilà, find myself immersed in a great presentation by a first-time speaker. The thoughtfulness and preparation ooze off the podium. And I'm entranced.

You're holding a book that will help your first presentation join the cadre of great performances. Even if you've given presentations before, Russ and Samantha have many, many techniques and hints you can take advantage of.

As you read the book, start to think about what'll make your presentation great. Think about the story you'll tell. Have you brought your own point of view to the forefront? Have you told us what your journey was, highlighting both the peaks and the valleys? Do you have a solid beginning, middle, and end?

And what about your direction? Do you know what points you'll emphasize? Do you have quiet, slower moments that give the audience a chance to reflect on the points you've just made? Is your passion coming through or are you holding back?

Read Russ and Samantha's wisdom, and imagine what your performance will be like. Don't be worried if you start to get nervous. We all get nervous. (Come visit me ten minutes before I walk on a stage, and you'll see me working hard to keep my nerves from getting to me.) It's how you know you're doing it right.

All this work and preparation is completely worth it. When you've done it well, it will help your personal brand. Folks will approach you about coming to work for them, even if you're happy where you are and not looking to move.

It'll also help the organization you work for. Presenting cool stuff about how your team is tackling important issues makes everyone look good. Don't be surprised if someone comes up to you afterward and asks if you're hiring (which is great because it can be hard to find exceptional talent these days when you do have an opening).

And, probably most importantly, *it'll make the world a better place.* By putting your thinking out there, you get other people thinking about their preconceived notions. Even if all you do is help them confirm that they know this stuff, you're giving them the gift of confidence. We all can use a little more confidence some days.

You're very brave to explore the wonderful world of giving presentations. I hope you're excited about it, because I certainly am. I can't wait to plop myself in the chair at your first session and hear what you have to tell the audience. It's why I came to the conference.

Go out and be an awesome presenter.

Jared M. Spool, Founding Principal, User Interface Engineering
Andover, Massachusetts

# Introduction

*Getting up on stage and giving a great presentation is easy!*

—No one. Ever.

Congratulations! You have taken the big leap toward getting up on stage in front of a live audience, and that's no small feat. This is a big moment! Savor it, revel in it, and acknowledge yourself for how brave you are—you've just made a commitment to do something that, for many people, ranks as one of their biggest fears.

When you present a topic to a group of people, you're starting to own your perspective about it. You're creating your unique view and sharing it with the world, and that's impressive.

If you're feeling a little uncomfortable, well, you're probably not yet uncomfortable enough. When you've got a room full of eyes watching your every movement, it can be daunting. In this book we hope we are able to share enough of our experiences—and the experiences of some other people who know a thing or two about presenting—from on the stage and behind the scenes, to get you to the point where it's a lot less daunting.

Presenting at a conference is a pretty compelling thing. There's great joy in the feeling of finishing a strong talk, particularly when you're in a line-up of other presenters that you're a big fan of. And up until that moment, there can be a lot of great stress, too. Knowing that, many of us still jump at the chance to get there and share the interesting things we've learned.

We're very excited that you've chosen to try your hand at presenting—in part because it's always great to see people trying new things, and in part because we hope we have the opportunity to be in your audience and become your fans.

In this book we will walk you through a variety of tips and techniques that can help you find your way to presenting at conferences. We start at the onset of the spark of your first big idea—and, in fact, we'll even help you find that first big idea if you haven't already! While we have each presented regularly and have felt successful to some degree, we've also had our share of bombs. And we still get back on the horse.

We've each had:

- Presentation submissions that were rejected by conferences we really wanted to speak at. Repeatedly.

- Presentations that started with a good idea but weren't structured well and ended up rambling or confusing. And people told us about it.

- Presentations that were underrehearsed, that had technical challenges, poorly designed slides, or no clear ending, or that went over or under the time limit. And we still encounter these things.

We set out to share some of our mistakes and the hard-earned lessons that we've learned along the way. We've asked some pretty brilliant people to share some of their experiences and opinions as well, in order to help you get started presenting as quickly, easily, and successfully as possible.

One more thing: It's helpful to remember that there are a lot more people submitting proposals to conferences than there are spots to be filled. Rejection doesn't mean that your idea or content isn't good enough; it might just mean that the competition was fierce and your topic didn't fit as well as other ideas that were submitted. Don't give up—revisit your content and try again somewhere else! There are a lot of great options out there, from local meet-ups to national and international conferences, and by doing a little research, you can find great potential venues for your presentation.

> **NOTE** If you're not sure where you can submit your ideas, Lanyrd.com is a great resource for seeking out conferences.

## Why We Wrote This Book

This book is not going to make you a great presenter.

You're going to have to do that.

The great ones, well, they make it look effortless. That's why they're great—they wow you, with brilliant facts, great stories, and beautiful slides, and they manage to somehow make you feel as if you're a part of a conversation with them. And frankly, we aspire to be just like them, too. We're lucky; a bunch of those great presenters shared their thoughts with us—as did some of the planners of the best conferences around—and that helped us shape what turned into this book.

This book, however, is going to give you some guidance and help you navigate the unfamiliar territory of finding the opportunity to get started down the path of presenting at conferences. We tried our best to share all of the things that we wish someone would have told us years ago when we first started down this path. We're fairly sure we still would have made a lot of the same mistakes that we've made; however, we probably could have made them a bit sooner, and we probably wouldn't have had to flounder so much to get to them.

We wrote this book because we've learned a lot as we've been giving our presentations over the years and because we would have liked to have had a reference like this available to us. We also wrote this book because we've done work with new presenters—both through the Cranky Talk Workshops that Dan Willis founded and through wonderful conferences, like the IA Summit (http://iasummit.org), that put a serious focus on bringing new presenters and their ideas onto their conference stages. We can sincerely say that with each chance we've had to do that work, we've felt energized, excited, and very selfishly like we learned far more than we had shared.

Presenting to an audience is a gift. When your presentation is successful, you'll know it, and there aren't many greater feelings in the world. We've each been lucky to have known that feeling a few times, and we wrote this book hoping that we can help you find that feeling, too.

## Who Should Read This Book

We think that this book will be great for those of you who are just starting out in your presenting careers. You've possibly never even submitted to a conference before; or maybe you did and you were really unsure about what you were doing; or maybe you've given a few presentations and you wish you had a bit more structure to what you've been doing so far. If you fall into one of those categories, you're probably a good candidate for *Speaker Camp*.

We've also heard from conference organizers that this is a book they'd recommend to people who are getting started at presenting.

# 1 BRAINSTORMING YOUR BIG IDEA

Big ideas come from the unconscious. This is true in art, in science, and in advertising. But your unconscious has to be well informed, or your idea will be irrelevant. Stuff your conscious mind with information, then unhook your rational thought process.

—David Ogilvy

Every presentation has to start with an idea.

If you are a regular speaker who gets invitations to present at events, the event organizers might request that you speak on a particular topic to fill out the conference theme. But more often, especially when you first start presenting, you will be coming up with your own idea.

Your idea is the central linchpin of your presentation, and while it is possible to have a poor talk based on a good idea, it is very difficult to create a successful talk based on a bad idea. When you come up with that right idea for you, and for the event you want to speak at, you've completed the first step.

Maybe you are someone who has a hundred different ideas of what you want to present, and you've even sketched out a few or created some slides. Or maybe you are at the opposite end of the spectrum, and you know that you want to start presenting, but you have no idea where to begin or how to come up with a topic.

Regardless of where you are, this chapter is for you.

# A Big Idea

The idea is the beginning of your work on your presentation, and it is the foundation of the presentation itself. While you may be itching to jump into creating slides right away, we promise you that spending some focused time on solidifying your presentation idea—and making sure it is a "big idea"—will provide big payoffs when you give your presentation. The stronger and clearer your big idea is, the more smoothly the rest of the presentation process will go.

## What Is a Big Idea?

So what is a "big idea"? How is it different from a regular idea? Think of the word "big" in all of its meanings. The Merriam-Webster Online Dictionary, at www.merriam-webster.com/dictionary/big, includes all of these meanings within its definition:

- Large or great in dimensions, bulk, or extent
- Large or great in quantity, number, or amount
- Operating on a large scale
- Chief, preeminent
- Outstandingly worthy or able

- Of great importance or significance

- Magnanimous, generous

- Popular

When you begin to brainstorm your big idea, take any initial thoughts you come up with and think about whether they map to at least one of these items on the list. Your idea might be big in scope—maybe a sea change in terms of how we should think about design overall. Or it could be big in scale—a case study of how you tackled a large project or worked within a sizable organization. Or maybe your big idea isn't big in scope or scale, but it represents interesting non-profit work that is for a good cause.

Your big idea needs to define your speaking topic and your reason for presenting. It should be something that will ground your full presentation from beginning to end and that is interesting and compelling to your audience.

> **NOTE** There are high stakes riding on your big idea, so it probably won't be the first one you think of. Coming up with the right idea takes time and effort.

As you begin to muse on your big idea, consider the following guidelines.

## Big Ideas Are Not Tactics

You may support your presentation's big idea with tactical recommendations on how to accomplish the idea, but the big idea itself needs to represent all of your presentation recommendations. Your big idea is the umbrella that unifies your recommendations, bringing them together into one holistic statement or proposal. For example, if you want to present on your experiences moving from working as a user experience lead at an agency to working client side, you might wrap this into a larger umbrella of how to continue growing and advancing your UX career.

## Big Ideas Are Not Concepts

Concepts are generalizations formed from specific instances or examples. Big ideas are more than this. They may start with a concept that you have been thinking about, some patterns you have seen, or relationships that were previously hidden. But big ideas crystalize concepts into something new, something that is more than just the sum of its parts. They distill concepts and theories into beliefs. If you have been thinking about the concept of big data, for example, your big idea could take that one step further and present your beliefs on how big data can be used to drive a truly personalized user experience.

### Big Ideas Are Not Types of Presentations

You may be tempted to think of a big idea as the type of presentation you want to give. Instead, a big idea can often be presented in many different ways that can be viewed as types of presentations. Let's say your big idea is "Wireframes Are Dead." This is an idea that has already been presented a number of ways, so you would need a new take on it for another big idea. You could then explore different ways of and strategies for presenting that idea:

- Why Are Wireframes Dead?

- Wireframes Are Dead—Build Working Prototypes

- Wireframes Are Dead—How to Convince Everyone Else

- A Debate on Whether Wireframes Are Dead

And so on. Each of these will point you toward a different presentation.

### Big Ideas Are Simple Yet Profound

Big ideas are often innovative, either containing brand-new viewpoints or concepts, or providing a new take on an existing problem. Big ideas may be controversial, or they may echo new trends or patterns, but they should always be self-contained, easy to grasp, and insightful. Big ideas should make you and your audience think, providing an updated viewpoint or new ways to consider or work through a problem. The best big ideas inspire curiosity and excitement to hear more.

PHOTO BY JOHN MORRISON

### Meet the Expert: Jeffrey Zeldman, An Event Apart

[What is a big idea?] A genuine idea. A fresh take on a serious problem, especially if that problem is currently vexing some of the best minds in the business.

## Why You Need a Big Idea

On top of creating a compelling topic that your conference organizers will want to include in their event and that your presentation audience will be interested in learning about, the big idea helps with all of the aspects of the presentation creation process. The big idea provides you with four *F*s that are important for a successful presentation:

- **Foundation.** A big idea provides the foundational grounding for your presentation.

- **Framework.** A big idea establishes the structural framework for your presentation and criteria for later winnowing of examples or subpoints.

- **Focus.** A big idea ensures that you focus on the key knowledge or value you want the audience to get out of your talk.

- **Fit.** A big idea helps fit and position your presentation within the larger event context.

### Meet the Expert: Jonathon Colman, Facebook

There is some kind of balance between figuring out what the audience for a particular venue will want and what you find exciting. If you aren't excited and passionate about the topic, you won't enjoy all of the work that goes into developing a great presentation. For me, if I can't show you how to do it, it isn't worth talking about. I always make sure that my presentations aren't just about giving an idea but helping the audience make it real, giving them tactics for success.

# Creating Your Big Idea

You may have a topic burning in your brain that you are dying to talk about. Or you may know that you want to start presenting, but you are stuck for that perfect idea. Coming up with your big idea can be daunting, whether it's your first presentation or your 100th. But you don't have to just wait for that lightning bolt of inspiration to hit you; there are specific techniques that can help you to identify topics that best fit your style and experience, as well as to refine those ideas to best match the conferences or events you are hoping to speak at.

Just like any other creative endeavor, brainstorming your big idea is a key aspect of the process. There are almost infinite ways to brainstorm, and books like *Thinkertoys: A Handbook of Creative-Thinking Techniques* and *Gamestorming: A Playbook for Innovators, Rulebreakers, and Changemakers* can provide all sorts of exercises and methods. In the following sections, we'll share some simple tactics that have worked for us when brainstorming a new presentation idea.

## Make Some Lists

Your big idea can start as simply as a random list of topics that interest you (**Figure 1.1**). Because ideas somehow feel different on paper than in the quiet of your own head, it is useful to break out your preferred list-making tools and just start writing things down or sketching whatever pops into your head.

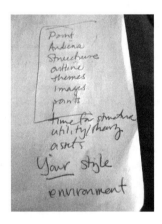

FIGURE 1.1 A really rough beginning presentation list around the topic of structure

While some of you who are more left-brain thinkers may not feel comfortable making a list away from your computer or without your favorite software or app, we encourage those of you who can stand it to start with a pen and paper for your lists. This seems to encourage free-flowing ideas and to help avoid getting too constrained with making it "right."

For the list making to be most productive at this stage, don't worry about staying organized or having a beautiful-looking list that someone else can read. Instead, you want to exhaust the realm of possible (and impossible!) thoughts you have had about your presentation so that you can start to narrow and refine these thoughts into your big idea.

# Focus on Quantity over Quality

Because at this stage you are working to note down everything you are thinking about your presentation, you want to focus on the quantity of ideas, not the quality. The goal is to empty your brain and put all of your thoughts down without judging them or worrying about whether they make sense.

You will likely notice your brain going on tangents, and that's fine—write those ideas down, too. Making this list, even if it contains a ton of really dumb ideas, will spark new ways of thinking that can drive even better ideas. Keep pushing to come up with as many ideas as possible.

It is important not to limit yourself to the first presentation topic that comes to mind! The goal of brainstorming ideas to present about is to help you extract as many ideas as you can muster. Then you can sort and explore. Identify the ideas that are worth diving into now, those that could use some additional exploration or time to percolate, and those that likely belong in the circular file.

## Try a Timer

If you are having trouble getting past the mental censor that we all have, or you don't seem to be coming up with many ideas, try using a timer.

In the process of writing this book and encountering writer's block, I read that legendary copywriter Eugene Schwartz used a timer to write copy ideas for 33.33 minutes at a time. After each 33-minute block, he would stop (even midsentence) and spend the next 10 to 15 minutes however he wanted. Then he started a new round until he had written for a little over three hours. This technique enabled him to write nine books on top of all of the successful ads, articles, and other writing he did during his life.

I pulled out my trusty iPhone timer to try it and was amazed at how well it works. For writing chapters, 33 minutes seemed like just the right amount of time in which I could focus without getting too distracted; and at the end of 33 minutes I could look forward to a little "treat" of walking around, browsing on the Internet, or just staring into space for a bit.

However, for making lists, try setting your timer for 3-minute chunks and writing stuff down with as much attention and intensity as possible. You will love how quickly your list grows.

## Narrow Your List

Once you feel truly tapped out and don't feel like you are coming up with any new or relevant ideas, you will want to narrow your list down into a manageable number of topics that you can then run through for further refinement. It may seem desirable to have the problem of too many ideas, but a large amount of options can make us uncomfortable and less inclined to make a decision. As the jam choice study led by Sheena Iyengar from Columbia University Business School illustrates, we can be ten times more likely to make a decision when the choices are limited.

Here's a quick process for narrowing your list of ideas:

1. Start by crossing off the ideas that don't make sense now that they have been written down. Ideally, you want to save these ideas for another time or another presentation, because sometimes a second look at a list of even dumb ideas will spur new ways of thinking.

2. Next, think about your background and expertise, and further winnow your list. There may be topics on there that you would love to speak about but that you don't have enough experience with yet. Save these for when you might have more experience.

3. Note whether there are ideas that you think would be interesting for someone to present, but you know that you just aren't the right person. Save these for sharing with friends and colleagues—maybe an idea that isn't right for you will be right for them.

4. Now discard topics that you think could be interesting, but you aren't passionate about. Even if you think it's a really cool idea, take anything off the list that doesn't get you truly excited. Creating and giving a presentation is a *lot* of work, and you have to be passionate about your idea in order to spend that much time and mental energy on it.

5. Finally, think more about the type of conference you are hoping to speak at. If you have targeted a specific one, review the description of the conference, the types of attendees it gets, past presentation topics, and any available presentation submission guidelines. If you aren't yet working toward a particular conference, spend some time researching conferences and getting a sense of where you and your background may fit best.

All of this information will provide you with some parameters for judging if your remaining list of ideas will fit within a particular conference or type of conference. Try to keep pushing until you have at least three solid ideas that seem within the realm of possibility for things that you could successfully present.

### Meet the Expert: Eric Reiss, FatDUX

I keep a list of things that I think are important. I spend a lot of time reading and watching things out of the zone of geeksville that everyone else is referencing. I try to find out what is going on in other aspects of the world. Also, because I'm older and have a certain degree of empirical evidence, I can see when things sometimes repeat themselves and can sense when the timing might be good to raise a topic again or look at it in a new way.

## Put Your List Aside

After spending all of that time thinking about the presentation, writing your lists, and narrowing them down to your best ideas, now is the time to put your work aside for a while in order to gain a fresh perspective. Depending on the presentation submission deadline you are working toward, this time may be anything from a couple of hours to a week.

After some time away, you may find that the idea you were most leaning toward is no longer your favorite. Or you may find a new subtle twist that suddenly transitions one of your ideas into a big idea.

# Refining Your Big Idea

Now is the time to break out of your own head and start to get some additional perspectives. Getting this feedback can be scary—after all, you have spent a lot of time so far thinking deeply about what you want to present about, and you are likely emotionally invested in your ideas.

# Get Feedback

The more time, brainpower, and heart you invest in a presentation, the harder it can be to view it objectively. This is exactly why getting outside feedback is necessary right now, as well as throughout the entire presentation process. When you are ready to get feedback on your presentation ideas, it is immensely valuable to get input from four different types of people:

- Someone who knows you well

- Someone who knows the event(s) you are targeting well

- Someone who has been involved with presentation curation or who has put on a conference

- Someone who is very different from you

It is possible that you know someone who fits all of the above categories, but it is useful to get different feedback from different people. This is especially true if you are tempted to just focus on people who know you well.

It is likely that the event you are targeting is run by someone who doesn't know you well, so having at least one or two people who don't know you well and can be unbiased at this stage will better mimic the situation you will be in when you submit your presentation proposal.

# Do Your Research

Once you have made tweaks to your big idea based on your external feedback, it is time to do some deeper research about the events you are interested in and what the conference organizers might be looking for in a presentation. At this point, you might be down to one front-runner idea, but don't neglect to do this final round of research and refinement work. This research will not only help ensure that you have the best big idea you can present at this time, for this event, but also will help you throughout the rest of the presentation preparation and creation process.

It may not be as easy as just looking at the conference website to find out the answers to all of your research questions. Try to glean as much as you can from that method, but if you know anyone who has attended the event you are targeting, you will want to enlist his or her help.

Even better is if you know someone who has helped organize that event. Now is not a time to be shy—successful proposals and presentations often require networking to provide you with the best intelligence for crafting a proposal and presentation that will suit your desired event.

## Know Your Event

The more you know about the event you are submitting to, the better you will be able to narrow your list down to one big idea and to hone and craft that idea to best fit that event. Here are some things to look for:

- **What language does the event use?** Think about whether you can better match your idea to the language of the event, or how the event seems to present topics that may be similar to your idea. Also note what kinds of presentations are common. For example, are case studies or how-to presentations more prominent?

- **Is the event more technical or more business oriented?** Will your presentation fit with the rest, or will it be an outlier topic? Either can be okay, but knowing where you stand will help with the rest of your presentation process.

- **What are the general timeslots available?** If most of the talks seem to be 20 to 25 minutes, you will want to make sure you can give a compelling presentation on your big idea within that time constraint. If the talks are more commonly 45 minutes or more, you have more time for a deeper presentation or a more complex idea. You might even decide to start with a 5-minute "lightning" talk to dip your toe into presenting, but even though you are on stage for a minimal amount of time, successful 5-minute slots can be just as challenging to prepare for as a longer talk.

- **What size is the event?** If it is a larger event, there might be different tracks of topics or types of presentations going on at the same time, which can reduce your audience to those most interested in your general topic area. If it is a smaller event, you may have a better chance of getting in as a newer speaker, as there might be less competition.

- **What topics have been presented in the past?** If a topic very similar to your idea was presented last year, you may have a harder time getting accepted unless you can offer a new perspective or a compelling case study. Looking at the types of topics an event seems to favor can also help you determine whether a more controversial idea would be accepted.

- **What types of speakers have presented in the past?** Similar to identifying prior topics that have been presented at this event, learning about which speakers have previously presented will give you a sense of what the event organizers are looking for.

You may have decided that there is more than one event you want to submit your presentation to, and that you can use your general idea for all of the events rather than submitting a different idea to each one. This is fine, but just like you would make changes to a résumé to highlight specific areas of your background or expertise that best fit each different job, you may want to make subtle changes to your idea to best fit each event.

## Know Your Audience

Next, it's critically important to know your audience as well as possible so that you can make the material most relevant to the people you would be presenting to. This is true for your presentation idea, your presentation proposal, and for the full presentation that you will eventually create. Being "user centered" from a conference audience perspective will help you create the best presentation possible throughout the presentation process. Some questions to research are the following:

- **How big will your audience be?** Preparing a talk for a 1,000-person venue at SXSW (South by Southwest, http://sxsw.com) can be very different from preparing for a 30-person breakout room at a niche conference. A larger event may draw a more diverse audience and may favor broader topics than a smaller, more intimate event. You can begin to estimate the potential size of your audience based on the size of the overall event, the size of the conference rooms at the event space, and whether or not the event is broken into tracks.

- **How much does your audience want to be there?** Try to find out whether it is an event that attendees' companies strongly "encourage" them to attend or if it is more the type of event where attendees lobby their bosses for permission to attend. This might give you a clue to their potential attention level and what type of talk might resonate more.

- **Who is paying for the audience members' attendance?** If it is an event where a substantial portion of the audience might be paying their own way (such as a discipline- or community-oriented event), it will be even more important that your big idea and the subsequent proposal is something that the audience is interested in learning about.

- **What's the knowledge level of the audience?** You will want to adapt the level of depth and complexity you plan to speak at to the expected knowledge level of the audience. If you are presenting to a group of students or newer practitioners, you will want to spend more time defining concepts and terminology than if your audience is made up of seasoned professionals.

- **What experience will the audience have?** Similarly, you want to have a sense of how much working experience your audience will have—both in general and within your topic area. If you are giving a talk on user research to a group of working customer insights professionals, you would provide a different level of detail than you would to a group of students.

- **What type of jobs will the audience members have?** Many of my presentations have been given to user experience designers and information architects. But I've also given presentations and workshops to audiences primarily made up of developers, audiences of marketers, and audiences of visual and industrial designers. Each time, I've adjusted my proposal and my presentation to best fit the expected core audience.

## Know Yourself

And finally, it's important to do some thinking about yourself, your interests, your expertise, and your style. If the refinement process hasn't yet narrowed you down to one big idea, spending time thinking about what you are most excited about presenting—and what you are most willing to put the significant time and research into creating a presentation for—can help you get to that one final big idea that you will be focusing on for the near future.

It is possible to speak on a topic that you aren't yet fully familiar with, and in fact this can be a good advanced technique for encouraging yourself to dig deeply into a new area that interests you. But if you are just getting started presenting, we highly recommend that you focus on an idea that you are very comfortable with and for which you can easily create content that you are familiar with. You don't need the added stress of having to learn a new subject on top of learning and honing presentation skills.

The feedback and research process outlined in the "Narrow Your List" steps should have helped you narrow down to just one topic to propose. If you are still struggling to choose between a couple of ideas, spend more time thinking about your passions and interests and where you most want to spend your time. While there will always be another chance to submit a conference idea, your first presentations will be most successful if you can focus on one big idea in order to give it your best possible attention and effort.

# Finalizing Your Big Idea

You should now have your one big idea—at least for this specific presentation. Take a breath and congratulate yourself. But you are not quite done yet. You need to spend some time refining your idea so that it has the best chance of being accepted to your target conference and so that the rest of the presentation process is as smooth as possible.

Consider this phase the "editing" one. You want to take your idea and describe it as succinctly as possible. Try to write down no more than one or two sentences that describe your big idea and why it's important. Once you have done this and feel good about the results, it's time to move to the next stage of the presentation process—Writing Your Presentation Proposal.

# 2 WRITING YOUR PRESENTATION PROPOSAL

The session title should clearly target the problem; the abstract should describe the problem succinctly, clearly, and authoritatively, such that every potential attendee the topic targets will grasp and immediately recognize that this is a real and vexing problem in their own work life.

—Jeffrey Zeldman

You have a lot to consider when you are crafting your presentation proposal. This means that you need to take the time necessary to think it through, let it percolate, and get it out of your mind and into the world. And then... well, then you're finally ready to give the proposal the additional attention it requires to become the masterfully written teaser for the story you want to tell.

You owe an investment of thought and time to your proposal—and also to the conference organizers and your audience. Don't do anyone, including yourself, the disservice of trying to cobble together what could have been a great presentation concept by pushing raw ideas into the form fields of a web page just minutes before the call for proposals deadline.

# The Standard Parts of a Conference Proposal

Every conference can potentially have a different approach to accepting submissions for consideration as part of their program. You may be required to provide audio, video, slides, or other media to demonstrate your knowledge and/or mastery of the topic. You may be expected to provide a list of questions that your presentation will answer. You may be asked for your gender, race, or other demographic information.

It's nearly impossible to predict what conference organizers will ask of you when it comes time to submit your idea. This is, in part, why it's a really good practice to start crafting your proposal well before the final minutes of the deadline for an event.

The good news is that no matter how much each conference may vary in what it requires for submission, at the core of almost every conference proposal are three very important pieces: the title, the write-up/abstract, and the bio. In this chapter, we'll focus on the title and abstract. (Chapter 3 will focus on writing your bio.)

## The Title

The title is your hook. This is the first thing that anyone reviewing proposals is going to read, and it's the first thing that's going to get that person to read your abstract with any degree of enthusiasm.

### Meet the Expert: Hugh Forrest, SXSW

For the title, be as detailed as possible within the framework of the suggested word length. Remember: Many proposals are essentially accepted or rejected on the title alone. A good title will spark my interest as a reviewer and make me want to read the entire abstract. By comparison, if the proposal has a title that isn't very interesting, it is *much, much, much* more likely that I won't find the proposal itself compelling—and/or that I will be looking for other reasons not to like the proposal.

You'll want to make sure that your title not only captures the eye of the people reviewing proposals but also your target audience. The title helps you get selected to present at an event, and it helps put butts in seats when it's your time to get on stage.

## The Abstract

The abstract you write tells the audience—and the reviewers—what you're going to get on stage and talk about. It's a summary of what people can expect to learn from spending their time with you, and it needs to inform them whether you're going to help them solve any particular points of pain that they may have.

The first job of the abstract, however, is to capture the eye of the reviewer. Even if your title has done its job correctly, your abstract has a lot of heavy lifting to do to keep the reviewer engaged, as well as prompt her to give you high marks.

### Meet the Expert: Barak Danin, UX Israel

I look for the value someone would get from attending the talk. In what way would they be more knowledgeable? What new "superpowers"—or, less dramatically, new tools—would they have after this talk?

The abstract completes the circle; if the title is your hook, the abstract is your melody. They need to work together and form a tune that people can't get out of their heads. The abstract will need to pay off the interest and intrigue that you generate with your title and help the reviewers get an idea of how your presentation will play out. It will also help the audience make their decision about which presentation to attend, as many events have multiple tracks or rooms with different presentations happening at the same time.

Members of the audience have a choice—help them choose you.

## The Bio

The bio is your opportunity to explain why you're the right person to stand up on a stage and talk about your topic. Many people, ourselves included, may get a little lazy and use the same bio for every talk. As you gain experience and expertise—and possibly notoriety—that may be more acceptable and forgivable. If you're just starting out and trying to get on stage to present for the first time, it's important to make sure that your bio sells the reviewers and the audience on why you're qualified to be there.

**Meet the Expert: Andy Budd, UX London, dConstruct**

You need to explain exactly why *you* should be presenting this topic rather than anybody else. So, is it something you've been doing for years, or something you've done for an especially well-known client?

Make sure your bio fits the topic. Don't tell the world you'll explain to them the intricacies of CSS3 and present a bio that talks about how you're a master of the lathe. All of the components of your submission need to work in support of each other.

# How To: Write Your Conference Proposal

Now that you know what the core elements of a conference proposal are, it's time to focus on the two pieces that are most tightly intertwined: the title and the abstract. These two pieces are significant because together they are what helps conference reviewers or organizers determine whether or not your content is a fit for the event they're building.

The more time you can invest in making these two parts work together and tell a compelling story, the greater your chances of finding yourself on a stage sharing your wealth of knowledge with an eager-to-learn audience.

## Developing Your Title

The title is a tricky beast. It's the first view into what your presentation is about—in many cases, you've not actually given this amazing presentation yet, and you may not have even pulled together your proposal, so a title can be challenging to come up with.

It doesn't have to be!

You've already spent a significant amount of time brainstorming your idea, or at least thinking of something that you're passionate to speak about. Take that brainstormed topic or that exciting idea and turn it into a temporary title. This title becomes what is known as your first-generation title.

### Meet the Expert: Hugh Forrest, SXSW

Take a lot of time working on the proposal itself—and proofing and reproofing and re-re-proofing. When you are satisfied that you have the proposal right, take the same amount of time—or longer—crafting a witty/creative/specific title that will spark my interest.

Think of this as a fluid process—for most people it is. The intent of your first-generation title is to merely solidify and give focus to the idea that you've got. It's perfectly fine to take the idea that you brainstormed in Chapter 1 and turn it into your first-generation title. It's okay to make it longer or shorter, as necessary.

> **NOTE** It's also okay if you want to write your title last. It may be easier to write your title later, but it may be more difficult to write the abstract without that focus point.

## First-Generation Title

When I've been thinking for quite a while or when the "aha" moment strikes about a presentation that I would like to give, I try to get *any* title together so I can start to find a focus for what I want to talk about. In a recent example, the topic is something I've been living for some time now—the transition from being a good designer to being a good leader of designers. I've been capturing bullet points of ideas inside of Evernote and sharing thoughts with friends and peers, and I think I know what this could be. And it all has been living under a placeholder title:

**"I'm a Good Designer and Suddenly I'm Leading People. Now What?"**

This placeholder has allowed me to keep my bullet points and ideas focused, and, if necessary, to determine which ideas can move to a parking lot where they may find their way back into the presentation or they may become their own presentation altogether.

Take this as a suggestion for getting yourself started, especially if this is the first time you're taking a stab at pulling your ideas together into a conference proposal. And remember: You've still got plenty of opportunity to make edits and/or completely throw out your title and come up with a new one—as long as you're not trying to assemble your proposal in your browser during the final minutes before the call for proposals ends.

## Developing the Abstract

It can be terrifying to think of writing the abstract before you've even gathered all of your content or created so much as a single slide (if you use slides). However, this is how it happens a lot of times. A presenter will have an idea that he wants to talk about, and he'll start to pull together his ideas, create a title and abstract, and submit them to open calls for submissions at a variety of conferences.

## Meet the Expert: Bruno Figueiredo, UX Lisbon

Start with a provocation and a brief overview of the problem, and then lay out your solutions to address it. Do not ramble on about framing the problem and then be vague about the solution. A short list of topics developed is useful.

A six- to ten-line paragraph is okay, or two to three paragraphs of the same length. Shorter than that tells me that you likely couldn't be bothered to write a good abstract, so it probably won't be a good presentation.

You're reading that correctly: In many cases, a presentation is created long, long after an abstract has been submitted to a conference. For many presenters, it's a bit like throwing a bunch of ideas at a wall and seeing what sticks.

We have a process we'd like to share with you. We consider this to be a great starting point as you begin your journey of speaking at events. As with many things, the first few steps of the journey can be the most challenging and the most stressful. Our goal is to help make those first few steps a little less difficult.

The process is pretty straightforward. That said, it's a little involved, and it requires a little bit of time and effort on your part, which, frankly, you owe it to your audience, the reviewers, and yourself to invest. We discuss this process in more detail in the following sections.

### Step 1: Shout. Shout. Let it all out.

When you begin writing your abstract, don't have a filter and don't worry about an ideal structure. Instead, take all of your ideas and turn them into two or three paragraphs that cover the most important details. You may feel uncomfortable, and you may find it challenging, but remember that this is your first draft and you're merely getting the ideas out of your head and into paragraph form. This rough content becomes your first-generation abstract.

### Step 2: You just walk away.

Save whatever you just wrote, and then get up out of your seat and forget about it. Go live your life a bit—for a few hours or a couple of days—however much time you need to come back fresh.

### First-Generation Abstract (Grade: F+)

The following is the raw brain dump of an abstract that I pulled together for submission to a conference. Keep in mind that it's rough, unedited, and, frankly, kind of awful.

And that's okay. (And it scares the hell out of me to share this with you.)

It's a first draft, and getting the ideas out is the most important goal for this first draft.

#### I'm a Good Designer and Suddenly I'm Leading People. Now What?

Finding top talent in the UX field has been a challenge for quite some time now. It doesn't help matters when we hear that there are several times more jobs than there are UXers to fill the roles, which ultimately puts the power into the hands of people looking for jobs, and they can now afford to be choosy about who they work for and where they work. This means that there is less tolerance for hiring a UXer to be the UX bandage and then have them report into marketing or some other discipline. Sooner or later, someone is going to need to lead and manage the UX talent pool, and that someone will need to be someone who has been in the trenches themselves.

Through the course of my career, I've had the opportunity to lead and manage teams, and I've not always been the best at it. I'm still learning, and I'll be the first to admit that. In many cases, my experience has been like most of my career: trial by fire. The good news is that I've been doing what I think you're supposed to do: get better through iteration, research, and adjustment. Much of what I've learned applies to managing UX designers, but it also applies to managing just about anyone, and I'll be sharing those with you.

### Step 3: You gotta come back.

After some time has passed, open up the first-generation abstract you created and have a fresh look at it. You may want to print it out and mark it up with a red pen—whatever helps you to identify the sections that need to be moved around, updated, or removed altogether. You may find an awful lot of copy that you wrote that... just isn't particularly good. This step is all about revising the content, and you should really start to pay attention to your structure, which could look something like **Figure 2.1.**

Here's what you need to tackle now:

- **First sentence:** Identify any pain point or problem you will help the audience solve when they attend your talk and put it right here. Support your catchy title with a strong, solid first sentence that not only keeps the reviewers engaged, but also gives them a very clear picture of what the presentation will be about.

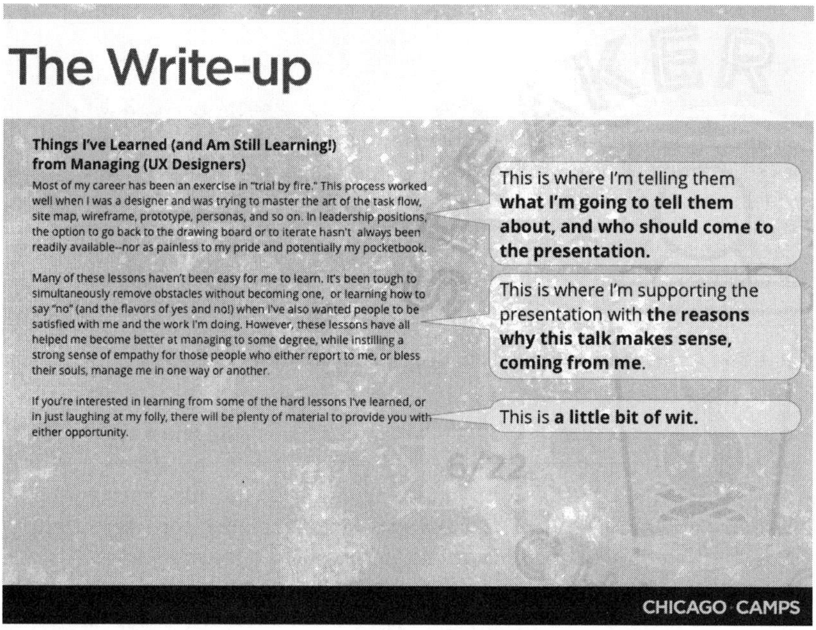

# The Write-up

**Things I've Learned (and Am Still Learning!) from Managing (UX Designers)**

Most of my career has been an exercise in "trial by fire." This process worked well when I was a designer and was trying to master the art of the task flow, site map, wireframe, prototype, personas, and so on. In leadership positions, the option to go back to the drawing board or to iterate hasn't always been readily available--nor as painless to my pride and potentially my pocketbook.

Many of these lessons haven't been easy for me to learn. It's been tough to simultaneously remove obstacles without becoming one, or learning how to say "no" (and the flavors of yes and no!) when I've also wanted people to be satisfied with me and the work I'm doing. However, these lessons have all helped me become better at managing to some degree, while instilling a strong sense of empathy for those people who either report to me, or bless their souls, manage me in one way or another.

If you're interested in learning from some of the hard lessons I've learned, or in just laughing at my folly, there will be plenty of material to provide you with either opportunity.

> This is where I'm telling them **what I'm going to tell them about, and who should come to the presentation.**

> This is where I'm supporting the presentation with **the reasons why this talk makes sense, coming from me.**

> This is **a little bit of wit.**

CHICAGO CAMPS

**FIGURE 2.1** The structure for the sections of your abstract

Not all talks will have this "pain point" or "problem," however. In those cases, identify the core theme of your presentation (the title/topic) and explain why you'll be talking about it.

- **Remaining first paragraph:** Reinforce your title and first sentence by continuing to tell readers what will be the highlighted areas of your presentation, as well as who should attend.

- **Second paragraph:** Support the presentation with reasons and rationale as to why this talk makes sense and why it makes sense coming from you.

- **Additional content:** Add more supporting details, and possibly a little bit of wit and/or personality, as long as it fits. Humor can be tough to pull off in the written word, especially if people aren't familiar with you and your style. When in doubt, leave the funny out.

- **The title:** Now is a great time to revisit and revise your title. Does it still make sense with what you've written? Can you come up with something better that fits with what you've written and that feels more connected?

Once you've done this, you now have a second-generation abstract in place, like the one shown next.

## Second-Generation Abstract (Grade: C+)

The following is an update I made to the earlier abstract after stepping away for a couple of days and putting the original out of my mind. You'll see a bit of an evolution, but I still haven't hit all of the points that I need to; nor have I fully identified the right pain point that I want others to relate to.

Note that I've also changed the title to more accurately reflect what I'm starting to see as the topic of the abstract and the presentation overall. It's still not there yet; however, you can see that it's evolving into something (hopefully) a little bit better.

### Things I've Learned (and Am Still Learning!) from Managing UX Designers

I've had the opportunity to lead and manage teams multiple times in my career, and while I may not have always been the best at it, I have picked up and learned a few things along the way that I try to put into practice today. Many of these lessons haven't been easy to learn, and sometimes they weren't that easy to endure; however, they've all helped me become much better at what I do, and they allow me to have empathy for those people who either report to me or manage me in one way or another. If you're interested in learning from some of the hard lessons I've learned, or in just laughing along at my folly, I'll have plenty of material to provide you with that opportunity.

Most of my career has been an exercise in trial-by-fire. This process may work well when you're a designer and you're trying to master the art of the task flow, site map, wireframe, prototype, personas, and so on, but with leadership, the option to go back to the drawing board isn't quite as readily available—nor as painless to your pride, and potentially your pocketbook. I'm going to share some of the things I've learned in my efforts to become a better manager of designers and in the world of business in general.

### Step 4: Who ya gonna call?

By now, you've spent a fair amount of time crafting the abstract for your presentation. This second draft likely has found you removing a lot of the cringe-worthy things that you wrote in the first draft and replacing them with more coherent and fitting copy. You've probably found a better structure that is starting to make more sense and that makes your abstract and title feel a bit more connected.

Now, reach out to a few friends, colleagues, or trusted advisors—the type of people who will tell you if you've got a booger on your face, not the ones who will tell you everything looks great because they don't want to hurt your feelings.

Find those people who will unabashedly tell you the truth and ask them for their precious time so that your content can become even better.

If they've got time to review your title and abstract, send it to them and ask for their critiques—and make sure to provide them with clear rules for critiquing. When left to their own devices, people will decide what they want to tell you and what's important to them, which may not at all fit what you're looking for. By providing them with some guidelines, you can receive focused and actionable feedback.

## Guidelines for Critiquing a Conference Submission

Here are some basic rules for critiquing a conference submission to help you help others help you. (Say that three times fast!)

### The Title

- The instant you read the title, did it make you think, "Dang, I want to see this talk!" or did you have to read it a couple of times to make sure it made sense?
- Is the title targeted to a specific audience, and can you easily discern who that audience is?
- When you read the title, does it fit the description?

### The Write-Up

- Is the write-up interesting, or did you feel yourself losing focus as you were reading it?
- Did it take too long for you to get to the key points of the write-up?
- Do you feel that you have a clear understanding of what will be presented?
- Does the description sync to the title?

### General Things to Critique

- Is the language used easy to understand?
- Can you read the content without needing to reread it in order to get the meaning?
- Are there any significant typos or grammar issues?
- Is any of the content too lengthy or not long enough?

(For more information on critique, see Aaron Irizarry and Adam Connor's website dedicated to critique at www.discussingdesign.com or their presentation at www.slideshare.net/adamconnor/discussing-design-the-art-of-critique.)

## Examples of Actual Critique

What kind of critique can you expect to get from your friends, colleagues, mentors, etc.? All kinds of it—and in a variety of different formats, too. In this case, I received feedback in a multicolored Google Document, an email, and a bulleted list, and each had some pretty clear, actionable items for me to focus on. Your mileage will definitely vary!

### Critique from Gabby Hon

I've had the opportunity to lead and manage teams multiple times in my career, and while I may not have always been the best at it, I ~~have picked up and~~ learned a few things along the way that I now try to put into practice ~~today~~. **Though the learning process has sometimes been difficult, each new experience has helped me become much more aware of both the professional and personal needs of people who report to me, as well as people to whom I report.** ~~Many of these lessons haven't been easy to learn, and sometimes they weren't that easy to endure; however, they've all helped me become much better at what I do, and they allow me to have empathy for those people who either report to me or manage me in one way or another.~~ If you're interested in learning from some of the hard lessons I've learned, or in just laughing along at my folly, I'll have plenty of material to provide you with that opportunity.

Most of my career has been an exercise in trial-by-fire, **and while that works well enough during deliverable creation, leadership calls for a much more organized approach. Managers have much less room to start over because** *(and here my mind goes blank: but what I'm thinking is that you have so many people and processes dependent on you, that you can't spin them all out willy-nilly)* ~~This process may work well when you're a designer and you're trying to master the art of the task flow, site map, wireframe, prototype, personas, and so on, but with leadership, the option to go back to the drawing board isn't quite as readily available—nor as painless to your pride, and potentially your pocketbook~~. I'm going to share some of the things I've learned in my efforts to become a better manager of designers and in the world of business in general.

### Critique from Brad Nunnally

I've had the opportunity to lead and manage teams multiple times in my career, and while I may not have always been the best at it, I have picked up and learned a few things along the way that I try to put into practice today. Many of these lessons haven't been easy to learn, and sometimes they weren't that easy to endure; however, they've all helped me become much better at what I do, and they allow me to have empathy for those people who either report to me or manage me in one way or another. *(This past sentence runs on a bit.)* If you're interested in learning from some of the hard lessons I've learned, or in just laughing along at my folly, I'll have plenty of material to provide you with that opportunity. *(This sentence feels like the end of the write-up.)*

Most of my career has been an exercise in trial-by-fire. This process may work well when you're a designer and you're trying to master the art of the task flow, site map, wireframe, prototype, personas, and so on, but with leadership, the option to go back to the drawing board isn't quite as readily available—nor as painless to your pride, and potentially your pocketbook. I'm going to share some of the things I've learned in my efforts to become a better manager of designers and in the world of business in general. *(Some of this feels like it should be in the center of the write-up; it's the hook that would lead to the end selling point.)*

## Critique from Samantha Starmer

- I would start with the second paragraph—I especially love the first sentence.

- I would consider taking out the first sentence of the first paragraph, especially if you start with the second paragraph.

- I would break up the second sentence in the first paragraph to separately call out the benefits of this talk on how you think about your own boss (vs. reports). That part really grabbed my eye because it isn't an obvious conclusion, and it opens up the interest of the talk to everyone—not just managers.

- I would embed a juicy lesson or two (maybe adapting one of your bullet points below) in the abstract to provide a bit of quick insight into what might be included in the talk and entice people into learning more.

Lots of really great bullets that I would want you to include in a talk on this subject— a few of my favorites:

- Do NOT be their knight, their parent; let them figure things out on their own, until you cannot.

- It Isn't a Measuring Contest; You do not HAVE/NEED to be the Best Designer on the Team.

- Remove obstacles and don't become one.

- Learn How to Say No.

- Learn the art of preselling your team's work.

## Step 5: Hit me, baby, one more time.

Once you've collected your feedback from your friends, colleagues, mentors, etc., take a few deep breaths and carefully read the critiques you've received. Receiving a critique isn't always easy to do, and it's essential to remember that your goal is to improve the presentation proposal you're putting together. The critique that you've received is meant to help you and give you a better chance at finding success.

Review the feedback, take notes, mark it up, put sticky notes on your walls—do whatever it takes to consolidate the feedback in a way that is useful and helpful to you. Then prepare what you think will be your final rewrite—and remember to update the title, too!

I have the advantage of having a whiteboard wall in my home office, so in this case I printed up all of the critiques that I received from my friends and stuck them, and my most recent version of the abstract, to the wall. From there, I went through each line of each person's feedback and started rewriting on the wall (**Figure 2.2**) until I came up with the final-ish version of the abstract.

**FIGURE 2.2** Rewriting an abstract on a whiteboard after receiving critique from peers

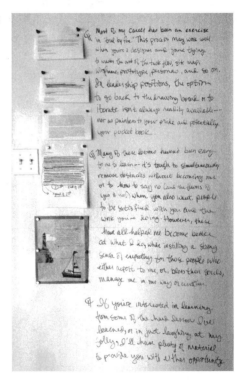

## Step 6: Push it.

Once you've updated the title and the abstract after receiving the critique, you could—and likely will—continue to labor over the way you wrote a couple of sentences, or whether or not you should reverse the order of this and that idea, or any number of other finer points. If you'd like to ask any of the fine folks who provided critiques to take "one more look" at your revision, you should feel free to do so. When you ask, just remember how many times you would want to look over someone else's awesome idea; don't make it a chore for those who provided a critique, and maybe they'll do it for you again in the future!

---

### Third and Final-ish Generation Abstract (Grade: B+/A-)

Based on the feedback that I received from some friends, I made a new round of updates that got me a lot closer to where I want/need to be before submitting this to a conference.

I've made more minor tweaks along the way to get to this version, including what I feel is a significant change in the title from "Managing" to "Leading," as well as the use of the parentheses. There is a lot of content that is specific to working with those in design, as well as content that has less to do with designers and more to do with leading others. These updates were critical.

#### Things I've Learned (and Am Still Learning!) from Leading (UX Designers)

I've worked for a lot of idiot managers in my career. And then, one day, after I had become a manager, it dawned on me: Now I'm the idiot! You see, most of my career has been an exercise in "trial by fire." This process worked well when I was a designer and was trying to master the art of the task flow, site map, wireframe, prototype, personas, and so on. In leadership positions, the option to go back to the drawing board or to iterate hasn't always been readily available—nor as painless to my pride and potentially my pocketbook.

Many of these lessons haven't been easy for me to learn. It's been tough to simultaneously remove obstacles without becoming one, or to learn how to say "no" (and the flavors of yes and no!) when I've also wanted people to be satisfied with me and the work I'm doing. However, these lessons have all helped me become better at managing to some degree, while instilling a strong sense of empathy for those people who either report to me, or, bless their souls, manage me in one way or another.

If you're interested in learning from some of the hard lessons I've learned, or in just laughing at my folly, there will be plenty of material to provide you with either opportunity.

At this point, you should feel comfortable submitting the abstract, as long as your bio (see Chapter 3) is also ready to go.

### Step 7: Ooh, ooh, it's never enough.

Don't be surprised if you find a typo that you were previously blind to, a new idea that would fit perfectly into your presentation, or even an altogether new structure or key points that would work well in what you've just submitted. After you've presented, you may find that you've identified new content and ideas as well. These are all okay—they're opportunities for you to continue updating your abstract and title. They may continue to evolve as you become more and more familiar with the content, and they should evolve so that your audience can get the best presentation possible out of you each time you present.

As you can tell, the process of crafting your abstract itself isn't all that difficult to follow. It does, however, require a bit of a time investment—a time investment that will hopefully have you putting your best foot forward and your best title and abstract into the conference's call for proposals.

## Tying It All Together

The title and the abstract should be connected to the topic that initially was generated as you were brainstorming ideas for a presentation. The title is going to be the first thing to capture a reviewer's or attendee's attention, so it is essential to invest time finessing it as you finesse your abstract.

It's also important to give yourself plenty of time to work through the writing and revisioning of the title and the abstract. Your ideas deserve enough attention to take them from that spark of an idea to a well-crafted and well-articulated title and abstract. Invest the time needed to prepare and give your ideas the best chance that they can have to be turned into a real presentation at a conference.

# 3 WRITING YOUR BIO

Tailor the bio to the proposal. If your proposal is about HTML5, then don't provide me a bio about how great a swimmer you were in college. Instead, give me a bio that convinces me you are the world's best expert on HTML5. Finally, don't assume that any of the reviewers of your proposals know who you are—and that you can essentially skip the bio portion of the process. Detail and specificity are your friends in this process.

—Hugh Forrest

Once you've got a title and an abstract that you're comfortable with, the final piece of the conference proposal puzzle is a bio that highlights your expertise and lets conference reviewers and your audience know that you're the right, most qualified person to be on stage.

Here's the thing about writing conference bios: No one really likes to do them—and in a very unscientific survey of a small handful of people, almost everyone will tell you that it makes their skin crawl to even think about writing one. Some compare it to the misery of listening to their own voices being played back to them.

And here's the secret: They're really not that difficult to write. They're about you, and who better to write about you than, well, you? It can be challenging, however, to know what to write about. Many people find it difficult to strike the right balance between presenting themselves as self-important braggarts or generic dullards. This is likely the second chapter in a row where you have a sense of dread about the task that lies ahead of you, and it's completely understandable—and that's likely why you're reading this page right now.

# The Two Types of Conference Bios

Here's another secret to conference bios: The shorter they are, the better they are. (And the better known you are, the shorter they can be.)

This means that your goal should be to get your bio as short as it can possibly be while still conveying your qualifications to the proposal reviewers and the audience. In order to make things really simple, there are two key types of conference bios to focus on: the short bio and the really short bio.

## The Short Bio

You already know the secrets about conference bios; now you need to do something about it. Let's begin with the longer of the two bios: the short bio.

The short bio is the one that you'll send along as part of the entire package that makes up the conference submission. There's no way to avoid coming up with this information, so you might just as well get started—how else are people going to find out that you're the right person to tell them what you're going to tell them?

### Meet the Expert: Jeffrey Zeldman, An Event Apart

Shorter is better. My favorite bio of all time is Martin Amis's: "Martin Amis lives in London." Of course, Martin Amis can do this because he is Martin Amis. You are not, so you do need to tell the world a bit more about yourself. But don't overdo. A good bio can be anywhere from 50 to 200 words, depending on the format of the conference website and the level and number of your accomplishments.

## Where to Find Your Bio Content

In order to create your bio, you're going to need to track down some information that helps describe who you are, what you do and have done, and how all of this history makes you an ideal person to talk about all the great things you wrote about in your abstract. Finding this information doesn't have to be difficult; you probably have a lot of it right in front of you.

Your résumé and your professional bio, such as those you may keep at LinkedIn (www.linkedin.com), are great starting points if you've been working as a professional for a while. If you're just getting started professionally, haven't ever written a bio about yourself, or are a student, it's a good idea to start collecting some information that will help you tell others about you and the noteworthy things you've been doing.

## Organization and Prioritization

Once you've gathered any information about you and the wonderful things you've done and are doing, you'll want to generate a list of your achievements and accomplishments—and don't be shy about it. I've found it easier to start by putting these in a chronological order—more a timeline at first, in order to help keep them straight in my own head (**Table 1.1**). I also start to separate my professional and personal accomplishments; this gives me less cluttered lists that I can easily cull through to determine what works best as a fit for the presentation that I want to give.

**TABLE 1.1** Sample List of Accomplishments

| PROFESSIONAL ACCOMPLISHMENTS | PERSONAL ACCOMPLISHMENTS |
| --- | --- |
| Coauthor: *A Project Guide to UX Design* | Teaching Daughters to Code |
| | 1976 Pong Champion |
| Coauthor: *Designing the Conversation* | Third Place Spelling Bee |
| | Pinewood Derby Car Design Award |
| Coauthor: *Speaker Camp* | Little League All Star |
| Coauthor: *Guerrilla Research Methods* | Excellence with the Lathe |
| Advisory Board for Harrington College of Design | Black Stripe in Tae Kwon Do |
| | Student Leader of the Month— College |
| Leading Teams for Several Years | Tuition Waiver—College |
| Authored Articles about Flash | |
| Rosenfeld Media Fellow | Fraternity Social Chair, Vice President |

Next, organize your information—separate the accomplishments that are related to your presentation from those that are not. Prioritize the accomplishments; you'll want to first identify the most significant items—the ones that are noteworthy accomplishments (such as writing a book, coining *AJAX*, or introducing Responsive Design) and move them to the top of your list. Then you'll want to remove those that won't help establish you as an authority on your presentation topic.

## Characteristics of a Good Bio

There is no reigning authority on what makes for the very best bio. In interviews with a variety of conference organizers, we found some overlap in what they're looking for; however, we also found that most of them identified unique elements that were important to them.

### Meet the Expert: Bruno Figueiredo, UX Lisbon

The best bios not only state a bit of the presenters' experience but also offer a glimpse into them as people. I love the ones that end with something like "has an unhealthy obsession with robots and loves to eat blueberry pancakes at midnight."

Here are some of the most stand-out pieces of advice that we've gathered from interviews with a lot of smart people who plan some pretty great events, as well as from our personal experiences. Keep these things in mind as you start to write your bio, and remember that this isn't an all-inclusive list. This is, however, a pretty solid starting point.

- **Write in the third person.** Someone else is reading this, not you, and forcing them to read a lot of "I am known for..." types of sentences can just seem awkward. Make sure your bio feels natural for the reviewers and audience to read.

- **Start off with your name and what you do.** Tell your readers exactly who you are and the job that you do as it pertains to your presentation. Make this your very first sentence. Feel free to roll into your major accomplishments immediately after your name and title. Pretend your readers are perfect strangers and lead with your name—make sure they know who you are before you tell them what you've done.

- **Brevity is the soul of wit.** Keep your bio brief; one to two short paragraphs or three to four sentences is enough. As mentioned earlier, shorter is better—and the more you become known, the shorter your bio can become!

- **Put your biggest achievements first.** You may need to kill some of your darlings as you focus exclusively on things that fit the proposal you're submitting to the conference. These achievements should support you as the right person to talk about your topic and should be related to what you're proposing to speak about. Remember: You're supposed to keep this short, so you'll need to cut unrelated accomplishments.

- **Write using common language.** If you're difficult to read, what makes you think that people won't expect you to be difficult to listen to? Unless you're speaking at a Mensa conference, you can expect audience members with varying levels of skill and education. And remember: Boring writer = boring presenter.

- **Spelling and grammar are of the utmost importance.** Don't rely solely on spell check, especially if you're prone to having difficulty with "you're" and "your." Ask for help, or, better yet, bribe someone for help with a nice meal. Who can turn down light editorial work on a full stomach? (Hopefully, not the person you ask!)

- **Clean up your language.** Yeah, that's right. Don't use swear words, and stay away from anything that might be offensive or vulgar to others. Know your audience and local customs and cultures as best as you can, and stay on the safe side. Don't be afraid to enlist the aid of the conference organizers to make sure you're keeping it clean.

- **Inject a little personal flair or wit. Maybe.** This doesn't work for everyone, but it can help make you come across as a little more personable. Make sure your humor resonates—when in doubt, leave it out.

- **Keep your bio current.** When you gain a new achievement or experience a life event that is important to you and/or relevant to the material you're presenting, update your bio.

- **Make sure you have easy access to your bio materials.** People who respond quickly to emails and requests for information might just be perceived as being easier to work with than those who delay their responses. Invest in some tools that can give you constant, ready access to your information, such as Evernote, Dropbox, or other services that are similarly easy to use, wherever you are.

- **Attach an appropriate headshot.** Get a professional photo taken, or at least get a really nice one taken by someone you know who is good with a camera. Some conference planners may prefer a photo on a plain background so it can easily fit into their website design.

Remember how you wrote your abstract back in Chapter 2? Take that same approach to your bio! Write a first draft as best as you can—let it loose and get all of the information about yourself out of yourself and onto paper. And get up, walk away and do something else, and then come back with fresh eyes and rewrite the heck out of it. Ask some friends (but not your parents; they love everything you do) for feedback and then spend the time needed to get your bio ready for submitting.

Now that you know what it takes to put together a great bio, let's look at a sample.

## Sample of a Short Bio

Russ Unger is an Experience Design Director for HF Money International, where he leads teams and projects in design and research. In addition to leading teams, he is coauthor of the books *A Project Guide to UX Design*, *Designing the Conversation*, and the forthcoming *Speaker Camp* for Peachpit Press (Voices That Matter). Russ is also working on a book on guerrilla design and research methods that is due out, well, sometime.

Russ is cofounder of ChicagoCamps, which hosts low-cost, high-value technology events in the Chicago area, and he is also on the Advisory Board for the Department of Web Design and Development at Harrington College of Design. Russ has two daughters who both draw better than he does and who are beginning to surpass his limited abilities in coding.

## The Really Short Bio

This is not a joke!

If you can create a short bio, you should also spend the extra time and effort to create an even shorter bio. Conferences vary in what they'll accept as the length of a bio when you're filling out their form fields. We've already focused on being brief and including only your most relevant achievements; however, it's time to chop off even more.

Keep it simple. There's no need to get into too many details for this version of your bio. In fact, if you can condense your primary accomplishments into general categories—such as by removing the titles of books coauthored and instead just mentioning coauthoring books on their subject categories—you can save a lot of space.

Try to get your really short bio down to a single sentence or, at the most, two very short, succinct sentences so you can be prepared for those situations where it is needed or required.

> ### Sample of a Really Short Bio
>
> Russ Unger is an Experience Design Director for HF Money International and has coauthored books on UX design and facilitation.

It's much better for you to be prepared with this really short version than to rely upon someone else to make edits on your behalf.

## Bonus: The Really Short Bio as an Introduction

In some cases, conference volunteers, a member of the conference committee that you've not met before, or a total stranger may be given the task of introducing you. They've probably done much less preparation for this than you have done for your presentation, and sometimes these introductions can come across as pretty awkward.

For these reasons alone, it's a good idea to have a printed and/or digital version of an introduction prepared so that someone else can handle the task as smoothly as possible. Here's an example that uses the really short bio as an introduction.

**Sample of a Really Short Bio as an Introduction**

Russ Unger is an Experience Design Director for HF Money International and has coauthored books on UX design and facilitation.

Today, he'll be presenting on lessons learned from leading UX designers. Please help me welcome Russ Unger!

# Bios Are Here to Stay

The art of writing the bio isn't one that many will confess to enjoying. Looking in the mirror and identifying yourself as an expert on a topic—or at least someone very well versed in it—can be challenging. You may be inclined to wait until the last minute and then just write whatever comes to mind without taking the time to plan your content and to align it to your presentation.

Do yourself a favor: Don't do that.

If you don't have a bio, start writing it now. You may need a bio for a variety of reasons, ranging from conference presentations to professional scenarios, to online profiles, to neighborhood newsletters, or to any number of other situations. Use the information in this chapter to get yourself started, and then you'll be prepared when you need it. If you've already got a bio, now's a good time to check and make sure it includes all of your most important, pertinent information.

Finally, keep your bio up to date, and make sure that it's current in all the locations where it may exist.

# 4 STRUCTURING YOUR PRESENTATION

Structure is perhaps one of the most critical components of a presentation. Without structure there is no clear narrative, and ultimately the goal of your presentation is lost. Structure is what can bond five seemingly random ideas together to form a powerful message that drives home the overall goal of your talk.

—Nick Finck

Developing the structure for your presentation may not feel like the most exciting part of the presentation process, but we promise that the rest of the steps will be easier if you dedicate time to this effort. Creating an underlying structure for your presentation will greatly assist with the winnowing and clarifying steps you will be going through as you refine your presentation. A strong structure can also help you avoid feeling overwhelmed by the effort of birthing a fully blown set of slides from the germ of an idea you are starting with.

Good structure doesn't just help with the presentation process; it also increases your likelihood of giving a successful presentation when your speaking slot finally comes. A strongly defined narrative and organizational framework for your presentation will keep the audience's attention, help them grasp any complex topics in your talk, and ensure that they take away your most important points. And solid structure helps you make sure that you end your presentation on time and on a strong note—there is nothing more disappointing than a presentation that starts off promising but fails to deliver a satisfying ending.

# Start with Your Presentation Goals

Before you even begin to develop your presentation structure, it is important to spend some thoughtful time clarifying your presentation goals. When you ask yourself questions about why and what you are presenting, as well as what you hope to accomplish, you will clarify your topic, its primary points, and what you want the audience to take away from your time together. Without clear goals, it is far too easy for your presentation to meander through the allotted time slot, leaving your audience lost or unable to recall the valuable points you worked so hard to convey.

## What Are You Presenting?

Start by ensuring that you are very clear on what you are presenting. At this point in the presentation process, you have identified your presentation topic and written your title, abstract, and bio. These are good first steps toward structuring your presentation, but remember that the process of writing your presentation abstract focuses mainly on how to fit within the conference submission process and how to get accepted as a speaker.

The presentation itself needs to build on this beginning work, but instead of being focused on the conference submission process and those choosing the speakers, it needs to be directed toward the audience who will be attending your session. Before you begin putting your presentation together, consider the following:

- What do you want the audience to get out of your presentation?

- If they were to remember only one thing from your presentation, what should it be?

- What should your audience be compelled to do after your presentation?

You should be able to answer these questions clearly and succinctly.

## Don't Panic!

At this point in the process, you may be wondering how you are going to fill all 30 or 45 minutes of the presentation slot you have submitted for. You may be anxious about having enough great material that you can confidently stand up in front of an audience and hold their attention for all of that time without resorting to tap dancing and bad impressions.

The reality is that most presentations allow for less time to speak on a topic than the depth of expertise you are bringing to it would permit and than the amount of material you probably want to cover would require. A successful presentation requires synthesizing a lot of background, experience, and expertise into a succinct capsule of information that can be crisply communicated in the brief period of time you will be speaking. (And from someone who has taught all-day classes many times, you would be amazed at how brief a period even a full day feels like when you get rolling. As Russ says, "Time moves differently on stage than in any rehearsal!")

This synthesis requires that you clearly understand and prioritize your main points. The added bonus of defining your presentation goals is that you will have already started the work toward building a great presentation that will perfectly fill your allotted time and that your audience will remember.

## Why Are You Presenting?

Next, get as clear as you can on why you are presenting. Unless you are very clear on why are you speaking and what points you want to make, your audience won't be clear either.

Knowing why you are presenting also helps you avoid the pitfall of being so close to your topic and the messages you want to convey that you forget that your audience needs to be brought along on the journey. They are attending your talk to learn something new, which means that they probably don't have the knowledge and background on your topic that you do. So don't forget to lead them toward the main points.

Clarifying "why you are presenting" should also help you understand your underlying goals for signing up for all of this work (e.g., to educate others on a topic you think is vital, to enhance your career breadth). Defining what you want to accomplish will help you fulfill the necessary steps toward a positive outcome. With awareness of why you are presenting, you can more easily determine what you need to cover so that you fulfill your presentation goals.

## Why Should the Audience Care?

And finally, it's important to specify why the audience should care about your topic, about your perspective, and about your presentation overall. The first two questions—what are you presenting and why are you presenting—help you gain clarity on the "what" of the presentation; this third question ensures that you understand and can therefore communicate the "so what" of the presentation. Knowing the "so what" will enable you to find the emotional hook of your topic and to begin to craft the structure and the presentation artifacts to support that hook.

**Meet the Expert: Andy Budd,
UX London, dConstruct**

You need to paint a picture in the minds of the audience, allowing them to imagine what the talk is going to be about, why they should care, and what they're going to get out of the experience.

Is it critically important that the audience starts making changes in their day-to-day lives or how they work because of your presentation? Should your audience use your presentation as an introduction to a topic that you want them to further pursue on their own? Or do you just want them to start thinking of things in a new way, perceiving their world from a different perspective that may slowly permeate their actions?

Understanding the "so what," convincing the audience that they should care about your topic, and helping them embark on whatever next steps are important will take your presentation from one of the ambiguous many that blur together in their conference-soaked brains and will turn it into the one that they not only remember, but that they talk about and take action on.

## What to Do?

All of these questions may seem a little daunting. You probably have a lot of ideas and thoughts floating around your head, and it can be difficult to translate them into anything concrete. The more concrete you can be with the answers to these questions, the easier the next phases of creating your presentation will be, and the stronger and more consistent your session will be when you actually give your presentation.

As with many of the presentation preparation subjects we'll walk you through in this book, breaking this task down into some specific steps can be helpful for tackling the work and making it more manageable. Find yourself a quiet spot for about 30 to 60 minutes and try the following:

1. Using your title and abstract, start writing short phrases that describe what your talk is about. Try to keep the phrases brief, focusing upon the biggest main points of your presentation. From this list, craft one sentence on what you are presenting. Make this sentence as clear and specific as possible—no run-on dangling participles!

2. Next, spend a few minutes thinking about what you want your audience to remember from your talk. Is there a central concept, methodology, or tip that you want to make sure they grasp? Out of these ideas, prioritize the one thing you want your audience to retain. Write it down in one sentence and consider using this sentence in your presentation.

3. Write down all of the reasons you are presenting: you always wanted to try it; you think your topic is so awesome that everyone should care about it; you want to get promoted and think presenting might help; you want to become more well known in the industry. Once you have captured your main reasons, spend a few minutes thinking about the order of priority. Which reasons are most important to you? Try to be as honest as you can—no one will see this. Write down your most important reason.

When you are finished, save this work in a place easily accessible from where you will most often be working on your presentation. If you get stuck during the presentation creation process, if you get confused, or if you feel like you have more (or fewer) ideas than make sense for your presentation, review your sentences. They will keep you on track and ensure that you are continually focused on your big idea.

At the end of the day, a presentation is a selling opportunity. You may be selling an idea, you may be selling a way of working, or you may be selling yourself. The better you can define what your perspective is and why it is important, the more the audience will follow along with you and be willing (and even excited!) to buy whatever it is that you are trying to sell.

# Build a Narrative

Humans communicate through stories. Whether they are told sitting around a fire, at a water cooler, in pictures, or in words, stories make up an integral part of our lives. While you may not automatically think of your presentation as storytelling, when you stand up in front of an audience for a period of time to share knowledge and expertise, that audience will instinctively listen for stories. Stories help us relate our different experiences and lives to each other. Told well, stories can trigger a deeper connection with an audience that ensures they will remember you and the points you want to make.

## The Narrative Arc

Any type of presentation is better if it has some sort of narrative. This doesn't always mean that you have to tell a story in the traditional sense, although relating personal stories that align to your presentation's main point can be a compelling way to gain your audience's interest. But even if you don't tell a personal story, you need to think carefully about the narrative arc and the beginning, middle, and end of your presentation. Let's take a look at the narrative arc (**Figure 4.1**).

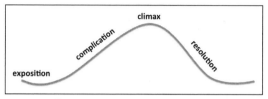

**FIGURE 4.1** The narrative arc

Your presentation needs to have a framework that creates clear markers for where the presentation begins (exposition), how and where the details that are generally in the middle are described (complication), where the turning point or lessons learned occurs, (climax), and where the presentation ends (resolution). This framework will provide it with natural structure, enabling the audience to follow you where you are going and to understand how you got there.

Consider how you will provide the background and description necessary to set the stage for your presentation. Think about the following questions:

- What level of detail is needed?

- How will you engage your audience's interest in the presentation topic?

- Is there is a complicating factor, a troubling issue, or some other tricky situation that needs resolution?

- What is the climax that can serve as the presentation's turning point, where your recommendations and their validity become clear?

Determining the benefit of your recommendations and how they can help successfully resolve a challenge will provide the audience with a satisfactory sense of completion that allows for a straightforward ending to your presentation.

Pull out the sentence you wrote earlier that defines what your presentation is about. This will help you create a clear narrative arc that stays on point and is connected to your topic. It will provide a strong common thread throughout your whole presentation that will ensure that all of your details, side points, or related stories back up that most important goal that you have committed to communicating to your audience.

### Meet the Expert: Eric Reiss, FatDUX

Storytelling is the key to everything. People remember the stories even if they don't remember the details. I've always thought in stories. This is why a longer presentation is easier for me than a short one. In a longer presentation, I can build the general structure and plan where the stories will come in, and I can adjust the timing as needed on the fly depending on how I tell the stories and how many details I end up including. In a short presentation, I don't have that freedom and I have to rehearse my words, how I'm going to tell the stories, a lot more.

## Provide a Beginning

Whether you plan it or not, the beginning of your presentation is where you create a first impression and set the audience's expectations for the rest of your time on stage. It needs to provide the background and set the stage for your topic. You should introduce any key players or details about the situation that are important to your topic and the later points you want to make.

Consider how you want to introduce yourself and any background or expertise you have with the topic you will be speaking about. Make sure this doesn't come off like an ad for you or your company! Usually one slide and a couple of short sentences about yourself or your expertise with the main point of the presentation is plenty. Your beginning shouldn't take more than about 10% of your presentation time.

Likewise, the rest of the beginning should be crisp and brief. If you start rambling without a point right away in your presentation, you may lose your audience before you even get to the meat of what you want to discuss. As you think about your beginning, make sure that you get the audience into the right frame of mind for what you want them to absorb and take away. You want to pique their interest in your presentation topic and in what you will be sharing, but avoid going into too much detail yet. Think about how much exposition and description you need in order to make your later points or recommendations clear.

## Meet the Expert: Dennis Schleicher, Sears

I usually go through three or four different ways of structuring a presentation. The way I first structure a talk is usually not the way it ends up being structured.

I still like structuring my presentation on index cards and spreading them all out on a big table. I can move whole sections around and see the big picture. It helps me eyeball what I am talking about and if I have balance between the different parts.

It's sometimes useful to think about structuring a presentation like planning a dinner, a five-course dinner—an appetizer, salad, soup, entrée, and a dessert.

And finally, it is helpful to think about what is your hook, or in Spanish *el gancho*. What is on the hook that is going to attract them to pull them in? I think for a while about that and if it makes sense with the structure. A good structure has references to the hook throughout the presentation.

Also consider what you want to ask of the audience. Do you have specific actionable recommendations coming later that you want them to pay attention to? Does a point you make or story you tell in the beginning get repeated for emphasis or progression later on? Depending on your style and the type of presentation, you may want to be explicit in the beginning about what the audience will learn in your time together, or you may want to build more slowly to the climax and resolution.

You may have heard the classic presentation structure tip variously attributed to both Aristotle and Dale Carnegie: "Tell them what you are going to tell them, tell them, then tell them what you told them." As you get started, this formula can be useful for keeping your presentation on track with your important points and can give you a path to follow. As you progress, it doesn't always have to be taken literally. Depending on your personal style that you determined earlier, you may want to use an anecdote, allegory, or even something out of the week's news to introduce your points, repeating them later with other stories or examples for emphasis.

**Meet the Expert: Jonathon Colman, Facebook**

The classical arc is "Tell them what you're going to tell them, tell them, and tell them what you told them." That is, an introduction, then your subject matter and content, and then a conclusion with the things you want them to remember. It holds for most talks, but it's interesting to play with. When I'm working on the structure of the presentation, if I can't watch the movie *Pulp Fiction*, I try to think about it so I can think about playing with time. Could I start in the middle or the end? How can I make the chronology more interesting?

And finally, the beginning of your presentation is where you make your first impression with the audience. Because it can often be where you are the most nervous, it can be useful to establish a stronger and more detailed structure for the beginning that you can easily rehearse. This will allow you to get rolling into your presentation quickly, getting your "presentation legs" under you right away. Most often, the bulk of your nerves will disappear once you get your presentation underway and get past the basic exposition points you make in the beginning.

## Craft the Middle

The middle of your presentation is where you provide the bulk of your recommendations, suggestions, thinking topics, or whatever the key points of your presentation are. A great beginning can capture your audience's attention and a fantastic ending can make them cheer for you when you are done, but the middle is where your substance needs to be; and a presentation without substance will only be remembered for its surface. You want people to remember your content and remember that you helped them absorb that content.

The easiest way to craft an appropriate middle for your presentation is to think about the following questions:

- **How many main points do you want to make?** If you have done a good job at answering the presentation goals questions we discussed at the beginning of the chapter, you should have a fairly well-defined topic that can then be broken out into some natural recommendations or points. For a 45-minute presentation, three to eight points is often most successful, but you might be able to get away with just one or two if your topic is more inspirational. Alternatively, you might be able to do more than eight if your talk is more tactical and instructional.

- **Do your main points have sub- or supporting points?** Or, put another way, are you going to stay big picture and high level and mostly be talking about your main points? Or is this more of a "hands-on" presentation where you want to provide a deeper level of detail? The more main points you have, the fewer sub- or supporting points you will have time for, so think carefully about which points are most important and fit best in the presentation.

- **How complex is your topic?** If your topic is very complex or technical, consider tackling just a couple of main points so that you can go into appropriate depth with the sub-/supporting points and any explanations or definitions you need to provide. It is more valuable for your audience to fully follow along and grasp each of the three points you are discussing than to get lost or overwhelmed and only remember three points from the ten that you talked about.

- **How much time do you have?** You only have a limited amount of time to give your presentation, and while there are occasionally presentations that can be somewhat successful by racing through "50 Tips for Good eCommerce Websites," for example, you will likely get more retention and attention from your audience if you limit your number of points and their depth according to the time slot.

## Don't Overwhelm Your Audience!

I once gave a 40-minute presentation with 12 main points, and each main point had two or three subpoints. In retrospect, that was too many for the audience to digest and too many for me to present well. I found myself rushing and not able to have the freedom to explore some of the more interesting subpoints; instead, I was forced to stick to a rather bland description of each point. It may have been a dense presentation, but I don't think it was a very rich or memorable one.

Also remember that complexity can apply to non-technical topics. In this example, the presentation wasn't technical at all. The topic was more of a big-picture, new-idea one, and I was introducing a number of concepts that were new for many audience members. Simplifying it by reducing the number of points I was trying to cover would have made the presentation more successful and could have left the audience wanting more rather than probably feeling run over by a truck after my dash through all 30 points.

The middle should be the lengthiest section of your presentation and is where you get into the most detail and examples. There isn't a hard-and-fast rule on how much time you should spend in the middle, but a good guideline is that the middle should make up at least 75 percent of your presentation. For example, if you have a 45-minute presentation slot with time for questions included, you will want the middle to be around 25 minutes, allowing 5 minutes for questions, 5 minutes for your beginning, and 10 minutes for your ending.

As you think about the middle of your presentation, pay attention to where you are trying to go; start to envision the end of your presentation so that you can make sure that the middle gets you to your desired ending. In fact, when you start creating your presentation, you may find yourself wanting to head to the ending while you are still working on the middle—this is fine! Just remember to return to the middle for as long as you need to in order to make it the true star of your presentation.

## Get to the Climax

Just like in traditional storytelling, the climax is the high point of your presentation—the place you focus your energy and content toward getting to in order to provide that sense of payoff and reward for your audience. It should be the highest peak of tension within your presentation, where everything you have been building toward culminates into your big idea. It is the peak of your performance, and a strong climax can ensure that your audience remembers you and your presentation.

You may be wondering how you incorporate a climax into what may initially seem to be a dry technical topic. While some presentation topics may more naturally lend themselves to a big epiphany or exciting call to change the world, every well-crafted "big idea'" will have some elements that can be leveraged for your climax. As you work through all of the main points and subpoints that you want to include in the middle of your presentation, answer the following questions:

1. Am I proposing anything new to my audience?

2. Are any of my recommendations surprising or controversial?

3. Was there a turning point in my or others thinking?

4. Was there a problem that needed to be solved?

5. Does my topic include a resolution to a problem?

If you really think about your big idea and how you got there, the answers to one or more of the previous questions should be yes. Next, remember the presentation goals you defined earlier. Pull out what you wrote down for what your audience should be compelled to do after your presentation. Merging your yes answers with what you want your audience to do will provide a strong message that serves as the point of your presentation. Voilà—your climax.

## Define the End

Finally, don't forget to have an ending! One of the most common mistakes that newer presenters make is not having a clear ending that provides a satisfying wrapper to the presentation. Just like the beginning needs to set the audience up for what you are going to talk about and help get their minds in the right place to consume the information, the ending needs to wrap up any loose ends and give the audience something tangible to remember.

As you begin to structure your ending, it's another good time to pull out your answers to your presentation goals questions and remind yourself of what you are presenting, why you are presenting, and why your audience should care. If you have a strong middle to your presentation that sticks to and follows through on all of these promises, the ending will be the place to reinforce all of that work. The ending is often a good spot to explicitly tell the audience the one thing you want them to remember, even directly stating it on a slide, especially if you have a less linearly structured presentation where you may not have stated it throughout.

### Meet the Expert: Eric Reiss, FatDUX

If anything, the end of a presentation—ANY presentation—is more important than the beginning. I generally try to sum up in a sentence or two the main points I hope to have made. And then to give the audience a direct call to action of some kind. As far as possible, I try to motivate and inspire. I want to leave the audience experiencing a high note. I want them to feel that they are part of something and that their input and actions really do make a difference.

This doesn't have to actually happen on a slide. In fact, many ordinary business presentations will end with a "Next Steps" kind of list. But what you actually say can dramatically affect the way in which your audience tackles these next steps. If throughout your presentation you have shown them *why* something is important, you should have no problems hitting the right tone for a memorable, effective finish.

We'll talk in more detail later about how to handle questions if they are encouraged at the completion of presentations for the event you are speaking at, but another benefit of a good ending is that it will set you up for an active Q&A that is separate from your talk. You don't want your talk to fade into Q&A without an actual end to the presentation—this makes you look unprepared and is one of the easiest mistakes to fix.

And finally, when you think about your ending, you want your audience to know that you are done with your points, and that it's time for them to clap. One of the most awkward things in a presentation is when it piddles off into nothing because the speaker either ran out of time or neglected to create a specific ending, and the audience doesn't know if the presentation is completed or not.

It is generally appropriate to finish your closing with a strong statement, question, or call to action (script this if necessary), and then pause for two beats and thank the audience. Make your thank-you heartfelt and sincere—the audience has just watched you on stage for some period of time, and, with all of our diminishing attention spans, this is an accomplishment that we as presenters should be grateful for! Your thank-you signifies that your presentation is completed and cues the audience to clap.

In gymnastics, a brilliant performance from the beginning to the middle can all be for nothing if the gymnast doesn't stick her landing. Similarly, you need a solid ending in order for the rest of your presentation to be remembered in the most positive light. Don't be that man who goes over his time slot and runs into lunch, or that woman who didn't know how to stop talking. Complete your presentation, thank the audience, and wait for some applause.

Stick your ending.

# Create an Outline

When it's time for the rubber to hit the road and your proposal needs to become tangible, pulling together an outline can be your best strategy for identifying the structure of your presentation. For those of you who remember creating outlines in high-school English class with something less than fondness, don't feel too tied down to some official outline format that has all of its Roman numerals in the right place.

An outline is helpful to provide a roadmap for you to follow when you begin crafting your actual presentation (**Figure 4.2**). It enables you to jump into the next phases of creating your presentation fairly quickly, and helps you move toward a completed presentation without getting too overwhelmed with the amount of work ahead of you. Creating an outline helps you get crisp with your main points, and it makes sure that you deliver on what you want your presentation to be about and what the audience will walk away with. It also helps you filter out subtopics that, while appropriate to your topic, don't support the main thing you want your audience to remember.

And the best part about the outline is that it doesn't have to (and shouldn't) remain static. Blowing it up and creating subsequent versions will help you further refine your ideas and find the focus you need to build a solid, well-structured foundation to your presentation.

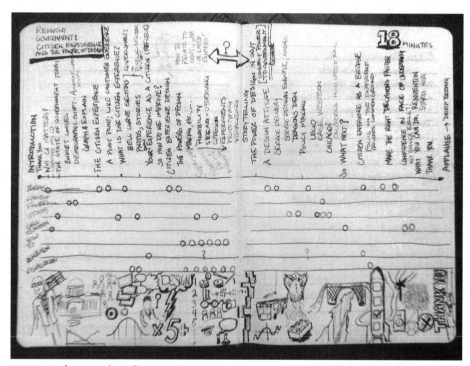

**FIGURE 4.2** An example outline structure

### Meet the Expert: Jess McMullin, The Centre for Citizen Experience

Structure is the tool that lets your presentation tell a story, make a point, connect with individuals, and inspire your whole audience (**Figure 4.2**). Structure is what connects individual slides and talking points into a coherent whole. And structure helps your presentation's ideas and feelings stick with people after you walk off the stage.

I think about structure like a music score or a recipe. Do I have the right notes at the right time? Do I have the right ingredients, and am I mixing them the right way? Those ingredients are the different kinds of approaches I might use, like sharing an idea, or making a passionate emotional plea, or presenting data or images.

For a new presentation, I start with an outline on paper. Then I check which elements each point supports: Is it about Ideas, Facts and Figures, Stories, Call to Action, How-To Instruction, a pause for Reflection, or an image or Visualization? I track each point in my outline against the kind of approach I might use. Like cooking or composing, I can see if there's too much data for this audience. Not enough stories? Need to pause? This lets me see the flow of the presentation and how I can reach individuals who respond to different approaches, like visual or verbal, facts or feelings.

Finally, I sketch thumbnail ideas alongside the outline to start planning the visual flow of the structure. By starting with structure, using it to plan the mix of presentation approaches, and then sketching, I can tune the presentation to the tastes of the audience and make sure my message connects with individual needs.

## Start Analog

There are a number of reasons to start your outline away from a computer, tablet, or other digital device. Working digitally tends to put people in a certain mindset that has been reinforced by years, maybe decades, of habits and ways of working while "at a computer." Even if you are using a mobile device, which may seem less constraining than sitting in front of a computer screen, starting digital can be too distracting to allow you to get to the level of quietness that drives structural clarity.

Digital devices include fantastic access to all sorts of resources that can help you research and create presentations, but this always-connected access is also what can keep you from focusing on the bones of the presentation, on the map you need to create to help you get to your presentation destination and ensure that the audience can follow you. This is why you can often make the most progress with creating an outline structure by finding a spot where you can concentrate for a few minutes and just start by putting pen or pencil to paper (**Figure 4.3**).

Don't worry too much at this point about your structure or level of detail; just note your ideas, your main points, and your subpoints. Keep this piece of paper with you as much as possible so that you can quickly jot down ideas as they occur to you in the shower, in the middle of the night, or while watching other presentations. As you work through this, you will eventually find a structure forming naturally that will help lead you to the next stage of a more formal outline.

If you are a more visual person, you may find the space and flexibility of a whiteboard or a big sheet of paper helpful for starting to carve out your structure and outline for your presentation (**Figure 4.4**). Another benefit of the whiteboard is that it can be easier to share with people and to talk them through what you are thinking about. Getting feedback at all stages of preparing your presentation is immensely valuable.

**FIGURE 4.3** Very rough paper notes that will eventually lead to a more structured outline

**FIGURE 4.4** An example of a whiteboard outline

As you start to build in more detail and get to a stage where you are reining in all of your diverse ideas and laying them out into a more defined approach, visualizing your structure can be very useful (**Figure 4.5**). Consider writing down each of your main points and subpoints on separate pieces of paper that you can shuffle around to better see the orders and structures that make sense. In her book *Resonate*, presentation guru Nancy Duarte advocates using analog methods such as sticky notes that can be placed on a wall or the floor to better "see" your structure.

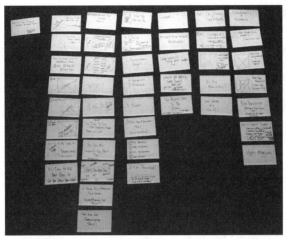

**FIGURE 4.5** An example of an index card outline

The more clearly you define your structure in these ways, the easier it will be for your audience to also grasp the structure and stay attached to the points in your presentation so that they can put it all together in their own heads and identify with what you are talking about. This flexible analog work can also help you start to tackle your transitions and notice where you can draw parallels and connections between things that you are discussing. These relationships will help solidify the presentation for both you and your audience.

## Determine Your Level of Detail

If you are speaking about anything that's complex or that might be new to your audience (and if you brainstormed properly as described in Chapter 1 you should have at least a new take on a topic), you will want to spend some time making sure that you've presented at the right level of detail. A good way to start this process is to distill the story you want to tell to its simplest form, and then gradually layer on detail and intricacy if needed from there.

Spend time thinking about how you would tell the story to your grandma. Or a child. How would you describe your topic so that each could understand and relate to something in her own life and experience? An additional benefit of this work is that thinking about how to describe something nebulous or technical to an audience who may not have background in the topic will help you focus on the most important aspects and not get distracted.

Don't worry about constraining yourself too much by your outline. Even if you are preparing a presentation that is less linear or that allows for audience interactivity within the presentation, some sort of outline will help you hit your marks and highlight the most important parts within your presentation.

## Move to Digital

Now that you have at least a general outline in analog format, you can start creating a shell of your presentation that will set you well on your way to all of those slides you have been obsessing about. One way to do this is to start by literally moving your analog outline into slides (**Figure 4.6**). It seems like a small step, but often just creating these placeholders will help you transition into what can be a scary part of the presentation process.

**FIGURE 4.6**  An initial digital outline represented in slides

Once you have created that initial digital outline in whatever format you will be eventually presenting in, you can use it as the foundational structure upon which you build the rest of your presentation (**Figure 4.7**). This will allow you to stick to the structure you have spent time planning according to your presentation goals. What's more, if you keep your initial outline-like slides in your deck at least until the very end, you will easily know when you start to go off track or add too much detail to a particular section, or whether you are missing big chunks.

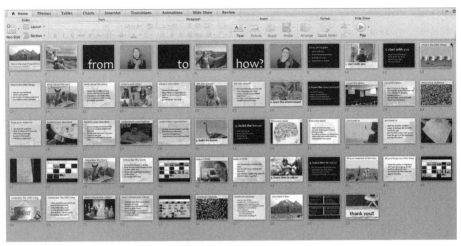

**FIGURE 4.7** The next version of the digital outline

You may decide to eventually remove all of the slides that "show" your structure—that is up to you, your style, and what will be most successful for your presentation. But keeping them in until you have almost completed your slide deck (or whatever visual tools you are using) for your presentation will keep you honest throughout the process and sticking to your most important points in a smooth flow.

# Ready for Creation?

If you have spent your structure time wisely, the creation of your presentation will be much easier because you have already laid out the scope and narrative and ensured that your main points and any subpoints are on track with your presentation goals. You will have already battled through some of your favorite, but potentially off-track ideas, and you will have put yourself in a great mental state to start cruising through one of the most fun parts of presenting—building the slides.

You will also be well positioned to start getting feedback on your presentation, because rather than a mess of pictures and barely started slides that no outside person can begin to make sense of, you at least have the foundation of your talk laid out in a structured way that makes it much easier to share with people. And while it is nice to hear compliments about the visual aspects of your slides or the pretty images you are using, the content of your presentation is really what you want the audience to remember. Sharing your outline in its various stages with people who will give their honest perspective will help them stick to providing feedback on the meat of your presentation.

And finally, if the dreaded technical difficulties that all presenters fear and hope to never deal with do happen to you—the projector doesn't work, slides get mangled, etc.—you should have such a strong understanding of your points and overall message that you could give the presentation without slides or notes at all. This means you could even tell your story in a strong and compelling way if you magically found yourself in an elevator in front of your CEO or your personal hero.

And that alone is worth the structure work.

# 5 CREATING YOUR PRESENTATION

There are three things I think about
when I actually build slides:
1. What do I need to say here—what
do I want people to think, feel, and
remember? Do I even need a slide?
2. How will this slide support that message
while keeping attention on what I'm
saying? I want people to pay attention to
me, with the slide deck winning an Oscar
for best supporting actor. People come
to see the speaker, not their slides.
3. What should the slide look like?
Presentation effects, like transitions or
animations, are like salt in cooking—
a little goes a long way, and too
much will easily ruin the best dish.

—Jess McMullin

Congratulations!

Soon you will be starting the creation of your full presentation and all of its supporting assets, including any visual materials, such as slides. For many, beginning to create the slides that you will use for a presentation can feel scary and overwhelming, as the possibilities seem endless. Don't stress! All of the great work you have accomplished thus far has prepared you well for this next step. And remember that there is no one perfect way to create a presentation.

Everyone has his or her own style for creating a new presentation. A few common methods:

- Jumping immediately into a slide deck tool to start creating master slides, including layouts, styles, and fonts
- Spending hours looking for the exact perfect images to use in the talk
- Writing out all of the story points and speaking notes for a presentation, saving the slide creation for the very end
- Methodically adding detail to an outline until the slides almost create themselves

As you get more experienced at presenting, you will find your own style and way of working. Building a presentation, developing the slides, and preparing any speaking notes is a creative process that you can (and should!) work through in the best way that stimulates your own creative juices. But in order to get you over the hump of the first time, we've compiled some suggestions that walk you through one straightforward way to create your presentation.

# The Slide Deck

Most conference presenters use some form of a slide deck as an accompaniment to their presentations. If you strongly feel that you will be more successful without slides, or you have another idea for how to give your presentation, it is possible to work outside the slide box. However, presenting without any slides can be challenging for those just starting out.

For better or worse, most conference attendees have come to expect some sort of visual information in a presentation, and not fulfilling those expectations can be risky. Depending on the type of talk you are giving, figures or images may be necessary to fully get your point across. It can also be difficult for first-time presenters to remember and successfully present 20 to 40 minutes of content without the assistance of slides.

An additional benefit of using slides is the ability to write speaker notes that can be secretly viewed by the presenter only via the presentation machine or "cheat" screen (**Figure 6.1**). This is an awesome tool for helping you remember what brilliant point you wanted to make while showing a certain slide, without having to load up the slide with too much text.

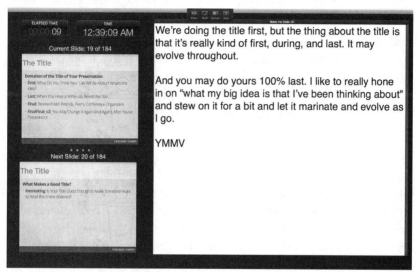

**FIGURE 6.1** A view into the joy of speaker notes

Because most of you will be using some sort of visuals, we will continue with the assumption that you will be building a slide deck. The next task is to determine what tool you want to use in order to build and present your deck.

> **TIP** It is possible to build your deck in one tool and present it via another, but because the tools don't always play nice with each other, adding this complication when you are first starting to present is not recommended.

## Learn Your Tools

Some conferences allow you to use your own machine—and therefore your preferred slide tool—for your presentation, but a number of them request that you provide them with your deck in a certain format. Find out the conference organizers' expectations before you go too far in your slide creation. There are few things worse than getting on stage and seeing that your builds don't work or your fonts are unreadable because the tool you used isn't supported by the presentation machine.

If you have more knowledge or experience with one tool or another, your best option will be to continue to use that tool, assuming that your conference doesn't require a particular format. You have enough new things to learn and get comfortable with right now—adding new technology on top of that isn't necessary and can just cause more stress. Similarly, if your place of work often uses one tool for internal or client presentations, you may want to just stick with that one so that you can continue to grow any existing skills you have developed.

If you don't already know any of the usual presentation tools, such as Keynote, PowerPoint, or Prezi, pick whatever one is most accessible to you and just start playing around. Depending on your learning style, it can be helpful to take an online course from a resource like lynda.com to walk you through the tools and buttons in whatever presentation software you choose.

## Keynote

Apple's Keynote (**Figure 6.2**) seems to be the tool of choice for the majority of conference presenters at user experience or design-type conferences—maybe because many of these presenters regularly use a Mac, and Keynote is the most convenient Mac presentation option. Many consider the graphic and typography capabilities in Keynote to be superior, but much depends on your ability and interest in creating new fonts or fancy graphics.

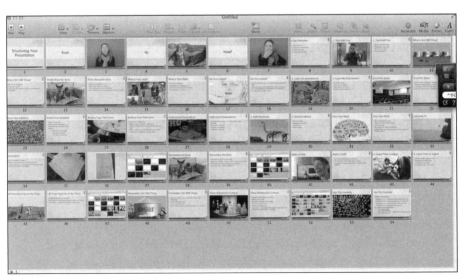

**FIGURE 6.2** Presentation on Keynote

Note that Keynote is not available on the Windows platform, while PowerPoint works on both Windows and Mac systems. You can export a Keynote presentation to PowerPoint format, but at times your fonts and formats won't transfer over seamlessly, which can create significantly more work for you.

### PowerPoint

Some feel that Microsoft's PowerPoint (**Figure 6.3**) does not support visually gorgeous presentations as easily as Keynote, but if you are more comfortable in PowerPoint (or on a PC) than in Keynote, your best bet is to stick with it. As simple as Keynote might be to learn, if it is your first presentation tool experience, switching and having to relearn and retrain your muscle memory can be frustrating and time consuming. If you are more comfortable in PowerPoint right now, you can always learn Keynote later when you don't have the stress of also building a new presentation.

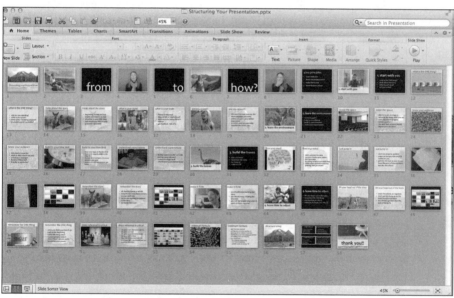

**FIGURE 6.3** Presentation on PowerPoint (on a Mac)

### Prezi

We recommend that you stick to Keynote or PowerPoint for at least your first few presentations. Prezi can be a fun tool to play around with, and I'm sure there are presenters out there who can give outstanding presentations with it. Unfortunately, it can be a very difficult tool to use well. Prezi is meant to offer a flexible style to support presentations that are nonlinear. However, the Prezi presentations I have seen live have generally left me a bit seasick and didn't seem to take full advantage of the nonlinear presentation style that is meant to be Prezi's strength.

### Other Choices

There are other tools that can be used for creating presentations—Google Slides, Impress, and Lotus Symphony, just to name a few. I've seen presentations given via PDF from InDesign files and presentations using just video clips or compilations—no traditional slides at all. I'm sure there are many other ways to create your visual backdrop, but Keynote and PowerPoint are still the most common.

## Continue Your Structure

Now that you have chosen your tool and started to get comfortable using it, the potentially daunting work of building your slides begins. It is very easy to get distracted at the creation stage of the presentation process. Even those of us who have created dozens of presentations can find ourselves spending hours on Flickr or Pinterest looking for just the right copyright-free visual representation of the word "ecosystem." (True story!)

Sometimes this kind of distraction can be useful for giving your brain a rest. But if you want to avoid that last-minute panic of having to build a full 45-minute presentation overnight (something that I let happen in one of my early talks), start by returning to the bones of your presentation: the structure.

The work you did in the last chapter will set you up well to make quick progress in creating your presentation. Take the outline you developed earlier and start filling in the details. You can begin simply by using each outline point as a title to a slide. As you begin this effort, you may find opportunities to tighten your outline.

You may also decide that you should more strongly highlight one particular section versus another one. That's okay, but if you go too far off track from your initial structure, you will want to spend some time reworking it.

Just remember: If you go too far along in building a presentation without that solid foundational structure, it will be much more difficult later to rein it back in. This is one of the benefits of spending time on the outline—it provides a road map toward a successful end of your presentation creation journey.

## Meet the Expert: Eric Reiss, FatDUX

I'll start by mulling it over for most of a Saturday. Then Sunday morning I'll get up really early and get into PowerPoint, starting at the beginning of the presentation. I already have the outline in my head and which are the main points, which are the takeaways.

I find it easy to create my presentation directly in PowerPoint. I get a lot of ideas just going through the grunt work of plugging in my outline and turning it into slides; it keeps the left brain occupied so the right brain can get creative.

Within a week, I have a pretty decent deck. In the meantime, I have been telling myself the story the whole week, which helps progress and clarify the narrative and the arc.

Of course, invariably you keep tweaking slides until the day of the conference.

# Hone Your Communication Skills

Once you have jumped into your tool of choice and have started to adapt your outline to a presentation format, you will want to shift your mind into somewhat less linear thinking and toward the matter of how to communicate. Presenting is just a form of communication. We get up to speak in front of an audience of strangers in order to communicate our thoughts, ideas, and experiences, so thinking about the best ways to communicate in this format will make your presentation stronger.

### Choose Your Visuals

As discussed earlier, most of the presentations you will be starting with will involve you speaking, with a set of slides or something similar as visuals behind you. This typical conference setup provides you with an excellent opportunity to leverage the power of visuals. Be careful of using too much text in your presentation, whether in bullet format or not. Always consider whether you could replace your text with a graphic, or whether one or two words might have more power than a sentence.

Great visuals can use all sorts of assets, including images, infographics, simple text with great typography, even working interactive examples. Don't lock yourself into what you find within your slide tool. Even if you aren't a Photoshop expert, there are a number of places where you can find compelling visuals for all sorts of presentation topics.

A word of caution: Be careful of copyright. Generally, it is straightforward to filter through a content set like Flickr for items that have been given a Creative Commons license that allow you to use the asset in a presentation as long as you attribute it properly. However, be sure to read the license rules for each asset you want to use, as they can change.

If you are having trouble finding something free to use that fits what you are looking for, there are sites like iStockphoto where you can find very targeted illustrations, photos, or graphics for a variable fee. And don't forget that you can create your own visuals! I don't consider myself an artist or a photographer, but usually a high percentage of my slides show images that I have taken myself.

## Focus on Data

While having visually compelling slides can be a big aid to a successful presentation, remember that there are other ways to communicate that can also effectively capture an audience's attention and help them to remember what you are presenting.

If your topic includes anything that can be backed up with data, don't forget to include that information. Well-positioned and appropriately stated statistics can draw increased focus from your audience. Researched and footnoted data can provide an additional layer of trust behind your words and help drive home the value of what you are recommending. Even better, well-stated data points or statistics often are the items most tweeted or otherwise repeated/shared by your audience, thus spreading your thoughts well beyond the original speaking space.

## Choose Your Words

While great visuals and persuasive data are very useful items to have on your slides (and may even make up the bulk of your slides), don't ignore words. While you don't want to put too much text on any of your slides, a few well-placed statements, phrases, or even single words can sometimes be the best way to hit a point home.

At minimum, it is often useful to have a few words on each slide as a title or other wayfinding marker to help your slides make sense to anyone who wasn't able to attend your presentation in person. In Chapter 9 we'll talk about iterating your presentation, but if you remember that your slides can have a life on SlideShare or in other places even after you complete your talk, it can help you determine which words will enable those remote, asynchronous viewers to also get value from your presentation.

As you choose which words best communicate your points, remember to also consider how the words look. Make sure you use a large, easily readable font. Nothing can kill a potentially great presentation more quickly than a font so small that the audience spends their energy trying to read a slide versus listening to you talk.

## If You Want to Go Deep

If you really want to dig into how to make the best slide deck you can, there are a number of great books out there on creating beautiful and compelling presentations. Nancy Duarte and Garr Reynolds in particular have created some standout resources on the topic:

- *Resonate: Present Visual Stories that Transform Audiences* by Nancy Duarte
- *slide:ology: The Art and Science of Creating Great Presentations* by Nancy Duarte
- *Presentation Zen: Simple Ideas on Presentation Design and Delivery* by Garr Reynolds
- *Presentation Zen Design: Simple Design Principles and Techniques to Enhance Your Presentations* by Garr Reynolds
- *The Naked Presenter: Delivering Powerful Presentations With or Without Slides* by Garr Reynolds

You can also learn a lot just by spending time on SlideShare and other slide-hosting resources and filtering the results by most popular and/or most liked. And of course, don't forget to attend as many presentations as you can if you want to learn more. Exposure to different conferences and presentation styles will help you define what you like and to find ideas that you can adapt and make your own.

## Remember Simplicity

As you spend time on making a visually compelling slide deck, don't forget that the core focus should always remain on you and what you are saying. You don't want your slides to distract your audience or worse, overshadow the points you are trying to get across. Think about communicating just one core idea per slide and keeping your visuals simple for maximum effectiveness.

Just like you don't want so many words on a slide that the audience struggles to read every word, you also don't want such complex visuals that the audience misses what you are saying because they are so focused on your slide deck. You can have beautiful slides but fail to have a successful presentation because you haven't communicated well.

While you may want to create the coolest slides ever, it is preferable for the audience to pay the most attention to *you* rather than your slides. As you become more experienced, it can be very compelling to make your slides actors in your presentation by adapting timing and pauses in your speaking to play up impactful or humorous slides. But this is difficult to get right when you are first starting out. If your audience is consistently looking first at the screen behind you instead of at your face, you might as well not be presenting live at all.

### Meet the Expert: Nick Finck, Amazon

- Start with the goals—what do you want them to walk away with?
- Build an outline of your talk, just bullet points.
- Each bullet should be a short story.
- Plan for Q&A at the end.
- Always cut the sales pitch.
- Never talk about the competition.
- Do not start with the history.
- Start with the end results.
- Tell interesting stories and entertain.
- Plan for about one to two points per minute.
- Reduce your outline by half.
- Turn bullet points into slides with images and no or minimal text.
- Make the font readable from afar.
- The first slide contains the name of your talk and the event.
- The last slide contains your email and/or URL.

# Additional Considerations

While building your slides, choosing your visuals and identifying your slide language will encompass the bulk of the work for creating your presentation, so the small extra effort of reviewing your deck with the lens of some additional considerations can provide a big payoff in making your presentation as professional as possible. Speakers who regularly present will often adjust their presentation to the specific conference environment and their own style, often continuing to revise and update presentations they have already given before to best match each particular event. Spending time on the following factors can make your own presentation more polished.

## The Environment

We'll talk in more detail later about how to adapt your live presentation to the environment in which you will be speaking, but even during the creation phase it is valuable to learn about your speaking environment and how to best tailor your presentation to it.

Certain types of presentations work better or worse in particular conference environments. It's to your advantage to consider some of those environmental details while you are still building your presentation so that you can sculpt it to best suit the environment. This will save you later from the last-minute panic of learning that the interactive session you planned won't be feasible in your assigned 300-seat, no-microphones-for-the-audience space. A few points to consider:

- **The Space.** Learn what you can about the placement of lights, screens, and the podium. The size and feel of the room will impact your audience's attention span and how easy or difficult it will be for them to remain focused on you. For example, a small room will likely feel more intimate and informal, while a large room may require bigger visuals and a more energetic delivery.

- **The Audience.** Try to determine what your audience will be like and what they will be looking for. Do they want to hear about results? Or is the journey itself more relevant? Will they want a technical or high-level presentation? What kind of assets will be expected?

- **The Time Limit.** Just as you considered your time limit as you brainstormed your big idea and began structuring your presentation, you will want to continue to keep it in mind as you build your slides and create your talking points. Remember to adapt the scope and level of detail in your talk to the time you are allocated.

Your conference organizer should be just as invested as you are in the success of your presentation, so he or she should be happy to jump on a call or email to provide any further information about the environment in which you will be presenting. For more on successfully managing your presentation environment, there is a great chapter in *Designing the Conversation: Techniques for Successful Facilitation* by Russ Unger, Brad Nunnally, and Dan Willis.

## Your Presenting Style

Understanding and adapting to your own natural style is a key part of a good presentation. While many of us have an inherent fear when we think about standing up and speaking in front of a captive audience, much of that fear can be reduced when you are thoughtful about your natural style and adapt your presentation to best match it.

One of the toughest presentations I ever had to give was to a board of directors. This was already a stressful situation, but what made it even worse was that the four of us presenting were requested to have a uniform presentation style. The slide format and structure had to be the same; our speaking style and speed had to be as similar as possible; our gestures and any movements were largely choreographed. My natural personal style is very different from that of the other three speakers, and although I practiced intensely, I never felt quite comfortable with how the material was structured and how I had to present it.

After this experience I realized how critical understanding your own style is for a successful presentation. I guarantee that it will be easier to plan and build your presentation, and you will feel more comfortable about it, if from the start you spend some time thinking about your natural style and adapting your presentation accordingly.

## Meet the Expert: Jonathon Colman, Facebook

A lot of speakers get too invested in telling the story of how they—or their company, or their product, or their client—are awesome. But there's a lot to be said for humility when speaking, especially on technical subjects. Some of my favorite speakers are humble in their approach and take great care to make their strategies or tactics as accessible and understandable as possible for their audience.

I think this approach does a better job at building community, driving engagement, and creating a bigger long-term impact than a speaker who tries to intimidate the audience with their expertise or technical know-how.

It may seem obvious that your natural style impacts whether you should stand in one place or whether you can get away with moving around the stage, but it may be less clear that your natural style should also significantly influence the structure of your presentation. For example, we've listed some style attributes below—think about which ones seem most natural to you and how you can use those traits in your presentation.

- **Formal or Informal?** Do you feel more comfortable with rules and structure; with introductions in the beginning and questions at the end? Or do you find yourself naturally meandering through anecdotes and wanting to get audience participation in the middle of your talk?

- **Big Picture or Nitty Gritty?** Some people naturally describe ideas from a big-picture, 10,000-foot view that emphasizes theory, wide-ranging possibilities, and inspiration. Others gravitate toward more detailed and tactical descriptions that instead focus on the specific instructional nuts and bolts of a topic.

- **Reserved or Theatrical?** Are you someone who is naturally dramatic when you talk? Maybe getting up to tell a story about your weekend, adopting your mother-in-law's voice for emphasis and acting out your niece rolling her eyes? Or maybe you find yourself more often as the one listening, saving your commentary for precise, to-the-point inputs that are more understated but can drive automatic attention.

- **Emotionally Relevant or Data Driven?** Think about whether you are more comfortable with sharing stories in an emotional way—for example, conveying passion, frustration, or optimism—or whether you are better with just the facts. Both styles can be equally compelling; what matters is whether you feel natural and comfortable.

While, as a newer presenter, it's important to understand your inherent style and to plan your presentation around it, don't feel like you will be stuck in the same box forever. When you are more experienced as a presenter, you can start to judiciously play around with your natural style and to try new things. You will have a better sense of what will work and what will be too much of a stretch and will come off as phony. Your additional time in front of an audience will also give you a better ability to adjust and recover quickly if you do try something that doesn't seem to be working.

## A Note on Humor

Don't try to be funny if it isn't natural. Many of us have seen people who are very entertaining or even hilarious presenters, and it is common to want to be like them. Few people who go through the trouble and stress of presenting wouldn't love to have all of that positive attention directed at them. But humor is a tricky thing and extremely individual. Have you ever noticed that one of your co-workers can get even the boss laughing out loud with what in retrospect seems like stupid jokes or observations?

If you are fortunate enough to be that always-funny co-worker, feel free to inject some humor into your presentation, but only as appropriate. This is critical. Even naturally funny people shouldn't try to make their whole presentations funny unless they are presenting at a comedy club. Humor is a great way to gain engagement, ease tension, and avoid boredom, but overreliance on humor if it isn't natural (or so well practiced that you can make it seem natural) can mask the true purpose of your presentation. Beware of leaving your audience feeling like they enjoyed themselves, but that was it—no other value added.

## Leaving Time to Adjust

Creating (and rehearsing) a presentation usually takes much more time and concentration than you expect. To make things more challenging, when you are new to the process you don't have a wealth of experience to rely on. It is important to leave time in your presentation process for your own editorial passes as well as for getting feedback along the way. As you gain familiarity with your own presentation creation cadence, you will learn more about how early you have to start (and how often and how long you need to work) to avoid that last-minute crunch.

My general formula is below.

1. Take the time allotted for your presentation slot.

2. Multiply by 5 = minimum thinking/planning time

3. Multiply by 10 = minimum building (in tool) time

4. Multiply by 5 = minimum dress rehearsal time

5. Multiply by 3 = minimum tweaking time

For example, for a 20-minute presentation, I probably spend

100 minutes thinking

200 minutes building

100 minutes rehearsing

60 minutes tweaking

And untold weeks stressing!

## View the Big Picture

When you are immersed in the details of building a presentation, especially if you are working on a visually rich slide deck, it is easy to forget about the presentation as a whole—whether the story flows well, whether the points are clear, and whether all of your hard work is supporting the presentation goals that you worked on in Chapter 4. In order to make sure that you don't forget about the big picture of your presentation, you will need to periodically lift your head out of the trees so that you can see the whole forest.

## Remember Your Presentation Goals

As you flesh out the details of your presentation, it is helpful to pull out the presentation goals you wrote down in Chapter 4:

• What Are You Presenting?

• Why Are You Presenting?

• Why Should the Audience Care?

The more you can keep your mind and your output centered on the most important things you want to accomplish in your presentation, the easier it will be to stay on track with a clear message and not get sidetracked with shiny new ideas.

### Continue to Get Feedback

Be sure to leave time to get feedback—a lot of it if you can. Certainly you want to get feedback from people whom you know well and trust, but try to stretch yourself to get feedback from others whom you may not know so well. When you present at a conference, your audience will likely include more people who don't know you than people who do. The more comfortable you can get with receiving a wide range of feedback—both positive and constructive—the better your presentations will be.

### Let It Rest

Finally, don't forget to leave time to walk away from your presentation for a while, ideally a few times, to rebuild your creative juices and let your ideas percolate. It is important to take a break from your computer and the slide deck so that you can return with a fresh perspective. It's difficult to do a good job editing and improving if you are exhausted and brain dead from working on it for too long. Get outside, meet some friends for dinner, or go see a movie. It is amazing how often a bit of time off can bring clarity and inspiration.

# Make It Fun

Creating a presentation is a lot of work, and you need to put in the necessary effort to make it the best you can. But don't forget to have fun along the way. In fact, the more you can find ways to enjoy the process, the more your enthusiasm and personality will show through, which will do a lot to make your presentation sparkle.

# 6 PRACTICING YOUR PRESENTATION

The best advice I can give for new speakers is to practice, practice, practice. I am guilty of hopping on stage with a new talk without putting enough time into practicing it, and every time I do, it ends up being a mediocre, uncomfortable talk. It doesn't matter if you're just starting out or a seasoned pro. A very well-rehearsed talk is key to onstage success.

—Kristina Halvorson

"Practice makes perfect!"

This saying is a great big lie that you should convince yourself to follow anyway, particularly when dealing with getting on stage and presenting. Practice does not guarantee—at all—that your presentation will be flawless, or that the audience will sit with rapt attention and adore it (and you for giving it).

Practice will, however, make you a lot less uncomfortable when you're on a stage or in front of a group of people who are convinced—based upon your well-brainstormed idea, carefully crafted presentation abstract, and wickedly awesome supporting bio—that this talk is exactly what they need to learn from right now. That is: Practice will certainly provide you with the opportunity to suck an awful lot less than if you don't do it at all.

No pressure.

# The Details of Practicing

We don't know many people who practice their presentations in identical fashion. Think about that for a moment. How in the heck is someone who is new to all of this conference stuff supposed to know how to practice their material if everyone is doing it differently?

It's a fair question. You see, many people presenting today have evolved their approach to practicing to a way that fits them—and to some degree, that is still evolving. When I practice, well, it's a constant part of the process—I'm writing down or speaking lines of content to make sure they make sense, and I'm asking myself "So what?" all the time. Sometimes I'll have the screen reader speak my notes so I can get an understanding of how that may sound to someone in the audience (albeit from a slightly robotic-sounding British woman). Sometimes I'll even have Brad Nunnally listen to my thoughts and ramblings via Skype and a screen share.  All of these activities go a long way toward helping me get familiar with my content and identifying patterns and groupings—and they're all part of practicing, for me. Or pre-practicing, perhaps.

### Meet the Expert: Stephen P. Anderson, Independent Consultant

I typically start with the opening and let the narrative lead me to what's next. This means "taking it from the top" dozens or hundreds of times, each time getting a little bit farther through the crafting of the presentation until I've reached a natural conclusion. I find that in the time spent structuring the presentation, I've also mentally rehearsed what I'll say, *ad nauseam!*

At this point, I will always walk at least one other person through the presentation, often in a partial speaker mode. This mock rehearsal is for their feedback, certainly, but also for me to get a sense of how the talk will flow. However informal, this mock rehearsal has always led to dramatic improvements.

This is part of my approach, and it is one that I've evolved into, and that I'm adding to and subtracting from for each presentation that I give. The more I speak to others, the more I learn that I'm not that crazy and that others have different tips and tricks that they use, too. This works for me, and it may eventually work for you, too.

In order to get to a mature evolution of your own approach to practicing, there are two things you should really focus on: knowing your material and knowing your timing.

## Know Your Material

No, really. Know your material as thoroughly as you can. This doesn't mean that you need to memorize every article, book, and blog post on the topic. It does mean that whatever you put in your presentation (and to some degree the material that you decidedly do not include) should be content that you're very familiar with and can speak to if and when questions are asked of you. (We'll discuss how to handle the audience, Q&A, etc. in Chapter 8, "Handling the Audience.")

Spend ample time with your material—be that research material, audio, video, or other media that you use in or that influences your presentation. Give all of your material your focus and pay close attention—take detailed notes as if you're in a work meeting and your boss is expecting you to be the scribe. Be as familiar with all of your findings as you would expect any other presenter to be with his when you're in the audience.

You'll need to be very familiar with the flow of your material and content, as well. If you go off track or your content appears to surprise you, an audience can pick up on it, and your message can become cluttered or jumbled. As Kristina Halvorson mentioned in the beginning of this chapter, any material that hasn't been practiced enough runs the risk of coming across as mediocre. This holds true for new presenters and seasoned professionals alike.

Keep this in mind: Preparing is part of practicing. And preparing well makes it easier for you to practice.

## Know Your Timing

Timing is tough to master, especially when you haven't had a lot of experience presenting in front of a live audience. Time passes differently when you're on a stage in front of an audience than it does in just about any practice scenario.

I know, for example, that I will take, on average, about one minute per slide or note card in a presentation, unless there is an activity or audiovisual component on some of my slides. I'm also really familiar with my own presenting style and pace, and I understand how much content I've included on each slide or note card. This has taken plenty of time (years) for me to get used to, and I'm constantly tinkering with content and delivery to see if it has an impact on my timing. I want to make sure that at my worst I end perfectly on time—although I've managed to go over more than once. At best, I'll finish with about five to ten minutes to spare to allow time for questions and answers with the audience. And if I'm totally off, I'll end 15 minutes early, or I'll end on time and will have skipped entire sections of content.

In addition, there's a limit to just how much people can retain over a period of time. There's also a limit to how much you can expect to cram into a time slot. Don't give your audience information overload; stick to a few key points that you want them to take away from your presentation. I try (and the keyword here is "try") to have one or two big ideas per ten-minute segment of my presentation. That's more than enough to keep an audience's minds busy, and it allows you to build content through stories, examples, and data, instead of trying to shove everything about a topic down their throats.

When you keep this in mind, it can help you further focus the material that you're putting into your presentation, which will also help you as you practice. The only way to get better at this is to practice and then to present in front of a live audience.

If only there were a way to perhaps do both things at the same time...

# Approaches to Practicing

There are a lot of ways to practice, and you will, over time, identify the method that fits with the type of person you are and the way in which you present. We've identified a few different approaches, as well as some handy advice that should help you as you get started down the path to presenting at conferences.

## So... How Do I Practice?

This is a great question! There are many opportunities for practice as you're planning and preparing your presentation, as well as once you've comfortably reached a place where your content is in order and practicing makes sense.

### Note Cards and Notes

You may find that you've got a bunch of material pulled together, but you're not yet ready to commit to it in the context of your overall presentation. Ask yourself, does it flow together correctly, does it make sense in a specific order, or does it even belong in this presentation?

I often practice before or during the phase of creating my slides in Keynote. Part of my preparation involves taking a lot of notes and iterating through them a few times until I'm pretty comfortable with the flow of the outline I'll generate. Then I'll create note cards to represent the slides that I think I'm going to need.

While I'm reviewing my outline and my note cards, I take time out to read through the notes to make sure that the flow sounds correct. I won't present as if I'm on stage and walking through each point; however, I will make sure that the flow feels logical by reading aloud each note or note card.

I find that this prepares me not only for creating slides, but also for giving the presentation, as it helps me get comfortable with the flow of the various sections. This increases my comfort with my slides and my content, and can keep me on track if I ever lose my thread in the middle of the presentation.

### Stop When It Breaks

Some people recommend going through an entire slide deck until you hit a point where your continuity breaks. Then you should stop, make corrections, and start over again from the beginning, repeating this process until you can make it through the entire presentation.

### Meet the Expert: Eytan Mirsky, Singer, Songwriter, Actor

I try to do some [content] that I am most comfortable with in the beginning because I know that if/when those go well, I will become more relaxed.

When it comes to building confidence in your material and making you feel at ease, this approach can work really well. Be aware that if you practice in this fashion, you may find that you're especially comfortable with the content that you have practiced the most: the beginning. Make sure you include some extra rounds of practicing to help you gain as much comfort with your closing material as well.

### Front, Front, Front to Back. Now You've Got the Knack.

This approach is very similar to "Stop When It Breaks," except that you don't stop when it breaks—you pause to take quick notes and then continue through the presentation in its entirety. Once you've completed the presentation, go back to the points where you encountered problems, make corrections to your content if you need to, and start over again.

This allows you to rehearse the entire presentation multiple times from beginning to end before you ever see an audience. The downside might be that you lose your presentation flow or rhythm as you continue all the way through or that your notes, upon review, may not be as clear once you've completed the practice run.

### Additional Approaches to Practice

As previously mentioned, different people have different methods for approaching practice. You will, over time, identify the way that works best for you. As you continually evolve how you prepare and practice, you'll find that those two phases often bleed into each other. In the book *Designing the Conversation*, by Russ Unger, Brad Nunnally, and Dan Willis, 18 different presenters shared their own approaches to practice; this is a useful resource for learning more about how others are doing this.

# And… Whom Do I Practice To?

No amount of solo practice really compares to giving a presentation on a stage in front of the real audience. When you reach that phase, time moves differently, and a lot of the things you wanted to remember when you got up there will have conveniently left the parts of your mind you thought you could contain them in.

In order to be comfortable and ready for this, try to practice in front of others as much as you can. Of course, the challenge with that is finding others who are actually willing and available when you are (finally) ready to practice.

### Practicing with an In-Person Audience

If you have the opportunity to practice in front of a live audience, you should jump at the chance! That said, practicing in front of any live audience still requires a bit of practice in advance—kind of like cleaning the house before the cleaning person shows up or brushing and flossing right before you head to the dentist. You want your dry run in front of a live audience to be at least a little pre-rehearsed so that the feedback you observe and receive is based on a version of the presentation that has some degree of polish.

Here are some options for presenting in front of a live audience:

- **Friends and family:** This is an audience that is good about once per presentation, so use it wisely. Friends and family, unless they've got a real connection to your material and to your successful presentation of it, well, they'll likely either lose interest, find something else that they need to focus on, or do their best to fake paying attention while tuning out and thinking about other things—which means that the value of their feedback starts to decline dramatically after a single round of presenting.

- **Coworkers and colleagues:** If you can find time during your workday and your employer supports it, schedule some time with a captive audience and walk through your presentation. Unless your presentation is work related, this group's vested interest in your success may wane after a first round of presenting. It may be helpful to frame this practice as an internal learning session for your team—"Lunch and Learn," "Brown Bag," "What Sue Knows About <Topic>," or the like.

## Meet the Expert: Dan M. Brown, Principal and Cofounder, EightShapes

When I think of "practicing" a presentation, I think of standing up in front of a mirror, or a select group of friends and family, and delivering the talk. The truth is, I don't do this enough. Even recording my presentation would be helpful, but I rarely carve out the time to do that. It's not ideal. When I stumble during a presentation, it's almost always because I haven't practiced delivering the talk and, especially, smoothing out the transitions.

Yet "practicing" could entail any number of rituals we do to increase comfort and confidence in the material. When my talks go well, I can attribute it to doing one of these things:

- **Rehearse small chunks:** My company gets together for an all-hands once a month. While I don't have 45 minutes during that time to practice a complete talk, I can take 15 minutes to deliver a section and get feedback from my colleagues. This dovetails nicely with my approach, which is to break a presentation up into three to four smaller talks (or more, depending on the length). By thinking of a presentation as a series of chapters, I can rehearse the portions in which I have less confidence.

- **Embed questions:** Audience participation is, I think, one hallmark of my presentations. (In fact, I mostly book workshops these days because I prefer engaging with a group rather than lecturing.) One part of my "practicing," then, is to insert questions for the audience into the speaker notes. If I lose my train of thought or find I'm moving too fast through my talk, I ask the audience a question, like "Can someone tell me a story about a project obstacle from a recent project?" This gives me a foil to make a point, makes the audience more engaged in the talk, and allows me to balance the timing. The added benefit? When "practicing," I can think through my own answers to these questions, again to build my confidence in the material.

- **Local meet-up groups, community, etc.:** Many local groups or communities of practice are always on the lookout for new content and new speakers. Identify these, and contact their leaders to share your abstract and bio and see if they would be open to having you as a guest presenter. These types of groups are typically more available in metropolitan areas; your options for finding the right one(s) can be limited when you are geographically challenged.

- **Standing in front of a mirror:** This can be incredibly difficult to do; however, it can pay great dividends. You can see how you stand in front of an audience; what your various "tells" might be; and what your odd quirks, facial expressions, gestures, and other things are that you might not realize you do without much thought.

- **Internalize flow:** Some speakers tweak their slides until the bitter end. That isn't my thing, but I do tend to walk through the slides over and over. I'm not actually speaking the talk, more flipping through the slides. This "practice" helps me internalize the flow, so I know the direction of the overall story. If something goes wrong during the presentation, I can take steps to set up the next part of the talk. During my regular session at the 2012 IA Summit, my slides crapped out. While I acknowledged that it happened, I restarted the computer without entirely losing the flow of the presentation.

- **Articulate key messages:** All my presentations have pretty detailed speaker notes, mostly because I believe I can write better than I can speak. At the top of the notes for each slide, I put a key message, the one thing I want someone to take away from this portion of the talk. If I lose my train of thought, I can always come back to that central theme. While this might be part of "preparation," I see it as a form of practice because I add them in after the talk is fully formed. Articulating them at this stage builds my confidence in the material.

- **Take feedback where you can get it:** My company encourages disruptive feedback—that is, interrupting colleagues to get some quick feedback. When I'm practicing a talk, I may invite a colleague to jump on Skype so I can walk through a few slides. Even piecemeal, talking through some slides helps me internalize the content.

When you put yourself in front of any live audience, you gain the opportunity to see how your material might fare in a real scenario, and this experience can be invaluable to you before you show up at a conference with your material for the first time. There is a different set of expectations at a conference, where attendees have spent their hard-earned money or their limited conference budgets to come learn from you, than there is in smaller, more controlled groups.

The comedian Chris Rock constantly rehearses his jokes in front of live audiences before he ever takes his act on the road or does a world tour. Rock will find places close to home where he can watch the smaller audience respond and react to his jokes—many of which will bomb many times before he gets them right. Sometimes, he'll have to throw away material that isn't working and that he can't get to work, and sometimes he'll find a home run where he wasn't expecting it. Either way, he's constantly practicing, making notes, and improving, and this should be part of your routine, as well. Practicing in front of a live audience can't be beat. Fortunately, there are still other options available to you.

**NOTE** For more information on Chris Rock's practicing habit, check out *Little Bets* by Peter Sims.

### Practicing with a Virtual Audience

In the event that you are unable to find a local group to present to, or if there isn't enough time to rehearse in front of one prior to your conference presentation, you still have options. Fortunately, the Internet, if you have access both to it and to others with access to it, provides some alternatives.

These options may prove to work well for you—they've certainly helped us find our way toward improving content that goes in front of an audience!

- **VOIP and screen sharing:** We love tools like iMessage, Skype, and others that allow us to reach out to a friend or friends who share our work and sleep schedules. There have been times when the combination of Skype (www.skype.com) and join.me (https://join.me) has made it incredibly easy to practice a presentation before it ever gets in front of an audience. Both tools allow you to share your content, as well as present in a normal speaking voice, for little to no cost.

- **Video cameras and audio recordings:** Most current versions of desktop and laptop computers come with audio and video recording devices built into them. You can also use screen-capturing software (QuickTime on Apple computers allows you to record your screen and any audio) to record your actions and your screen, so you can see and hear your presentation during playback. You can also go a little "old fashioned" and record yourself with a camcorder as you go through the presentation. Both of these approaches allow you (possibly somewhat to your own chagrin) to see and hear what you're like during a presentation. When you hear your voice played back to you it can be a shock, so steady yourself and don't press the stop button during playback—this is for the benefit of you and your audience!

As an added bonus: If you ever present in a webinar or virtual/online seminar where you won't be able to see the audience, these approaches to practicing can help get you ready!

# Practice Makes Better

Practicing can take some getting used to. You don't need to write out and memorize every single word that you plan on saying in order to do it. Many people will be able to tell if that's what you're doing, and they may lose interest if that's your approach. Avoid being a robot who gives the same presentation every time! Take each round of practice as an opportunity to become more familiar with your content and your behavior on stage. Know your mannerisms and habits, and be aware if they can become distracting to your audience.

Every time you give a presentation, it's yet another round of practice for the next time you present it. You may not realize it, but it's also practice for every other presentation after it as well. Each time you get on stage, you learn, you adjust both mentally and physically to the environment, and you begin to understand how to at least appear more natural when you're there.

Seasoned presenters will tell you that they still get nervous before presenting, even if you would never guess it by looking at them. It's not that it gets any easier; it's just that you become more used to it, and you become more natural, possibly more automated, at handling your material.

Remember, your audience wants you to succeed, and they want to learn from you and your experiences. You've earned your spot on the stage, and you owe it to the audience and the conference organizers to show up prepared. Don't miss your opportunities to practice and improve so you can give your best presentation each time.

# 7 PRESENTATION TIPS AND TECHNIQUES

I think nervousness can also be "preparedness." Nerves tend to focus me on things I need to remember...

Sorry, no real tricks. Just remember, there's a reason why you're up there on stage. You have to believe that reason yourself. Know your material and be able to answer anything.

—Christian Lane

There are no tricks when it comes to being a great presenter. You need to appropriately prepare and practice your material so you can be comfortable on stage in front of a group of people who want to learn from you. (You've read that at least a few times if you've read any other chapters of this book, and it's a mantra you should get comfortable with.) If you're reading your presentation from speaker notes or shuffling through stacks of papers or note cards, it can be obvious and distracting, so get yourself to a point where that's not a concern.

Be ready. Be prepared.

And then, when you get on that stage for the first time, there will still be more things to know that won't have anything to do with the content you've worked so hard to master. It takes a lot of preparation and practice, and it requires under-standing the environments you present in, the tools you present with, and the way you, yourself, present.

# The Pre-Game

We've been preaching that being prepared with your content is the best way to make sure you give your presentation well, and that's still correct. It is, however, not all that you need to consider when you're giving a presentation. You'll still want to do some additional preparation for your presentation, most of which can happen within the 24 hours prior to when you step on the stage.

## Know the Computer You're Presenting From

This might seem a little silly; however, there's more to presenting than just pressing the magical button that makes your presentation "play." There are a lot of things to consider, from calibrating your colors so that they look best on whatever display you're provided with (which can range from a state-of-the-art television set to an antiquated projector that hasn't had a bulb changed since before the 1984 Summer Olympics) to knowing what dongle you'll need so you can push video to a projector.

These are all things you'll want to practice and prepare for. Each computer may have a different way to adjust color, brightness, and other relevant video and audio settings. It's your job to know how these things work, and to make sure you test them and adjust for them so that your audience can see and hear your material as you intend it.

You'll also want to make sure that you understand how your material will present. If you've only got a laptop or a stand-alone desktop computer, buy or borrow an external monitor so you can see what your presenter view will look like, as well as the slides that you'll present (**Figure 7.1**). Learn how to update your presenter view in order to provide yourself with the best information while you're on stage.

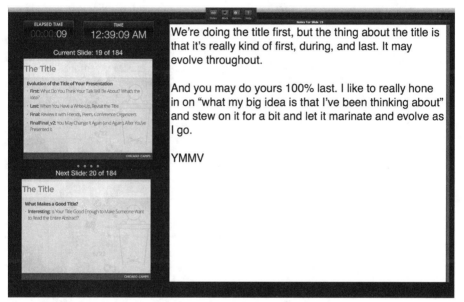

**FIGURE 7.1** My preferred layout for presenter view in Keynote for Mac

Invariably, each presenter will need at least a few minutes to get his or her equipment ready and displaying correctly on whatever output is available. It's easy to get a little rattled when things don't go as planned, and it's not unusual to have the display settings suddenly become invisible, even when they're in plain sight, and right before you go on.

If you know your laptop and you're comfortable finding the settings that you need to adjust, you'll be much calmer when you start your presentation. The more familiar you are with your equipment, the less likely you are to find yourself unsettled on stage, and the less likely an audience is to see you become flushed, hear your voice tremble, or see you sweat.

## Learn and Know the Tool You'll Be Presenting With

There are some people who can do really, truly amazing things with PowerPoint. They can make objects dance on a screen in a well-designed fashion that makes a lot of people in their audience ask them "What tool do you use?" Then, when the inquirers hear the answer "PowerPoint," they're shocked. But it's not as though PowerPoint, Keynote, Prezi, and any other tool that you might use are dramatically different in what they do, which is display your content on a screen.

Regardless of what software you choose, you should know it, and know it well enough to understand things like how to use the Presenter view, how to set up slide masters and styles, and how to handle some very basic transitions. It can be challenging to try to become proficient with a new tool while also preparing and practicing new content, so you'll want to make sure you give yourself ample time to work inside of your digital tool of choice (assuming that you'll be using one) (**Figure 7.2**). If you're using any presentation software for the first time, do yourself a favor and budget at least double the amount of time you think it will take you to create your slides.

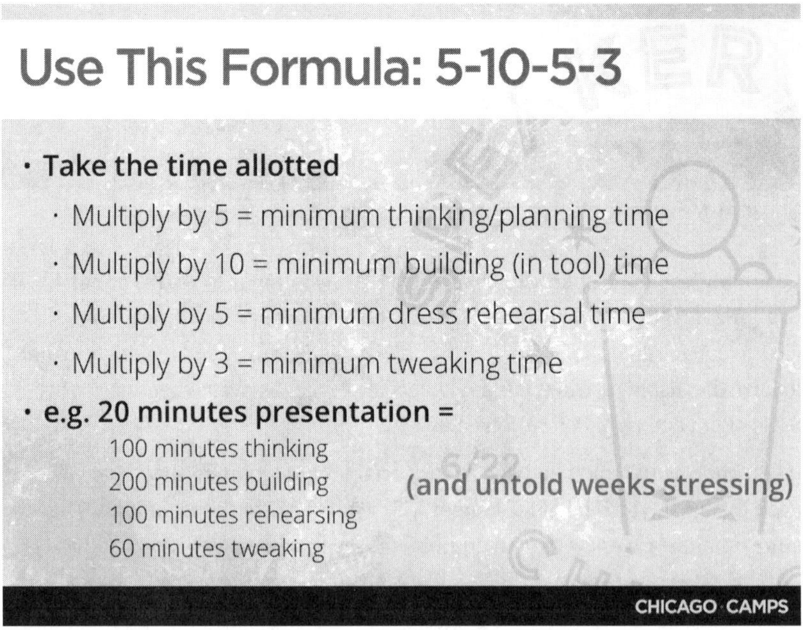

# Use This Formula: 5-10-5-3

- **Take the time allotted**
  - Multiply by 5 = minimum thinking/planning time
  - Multiply by 10 = minimum building (in tool) time
  - Multiply by 5 = minimum dress rehearsal time
  - Multiply by 3 = minimum tweaking time
- **e.g. 20 minutes presentation =**
  100 minutes thinking
  200 minutes building     (and untold weeks stressing)
  100 minutes rehearsing
  60 minutes tweaking

CHICAGO · CAMPS

**FIGURE 7.2** Samantha Starmer's magical formula for estimating the amount of time you need for preparing your presentation

**NOTE** Everyone has his own formula for how long slide creation takes. The only real problem with that is that it takes a lot of time, a lot of learning, and likely a lot of mistakes to figure that out. Don't find yourself in the mistake category, especially as a first-time presenter—there's plenty of stress happening for you as it is. Allow yourself a buffer.

I generally allow about an hour for each slide that I need to create. Some will take longer, some will take much less than that; however, that's my baseline figure. If an average talk is about 45 minutes, I try to time my content to about 35 minutes in order to leave time for Q&A. This means that a slide deck can take me anywhere from 35 to 55 hours, depending on how many slides I have. If I were brand new at this again, I'd start building my presentation about a month before my talk, which means I'd need to have all of my outlines and primary research handled before then, especially since presentations get built on my own time— not during my day job!

## Keep a Backup of All of Your Files

Computers today are awesome. They're faster than they've ever been, they've got great displays, and all kinds of magical functionality is buried in their operating systems. And they still break.

Invest in a backup solution, such as Dropbox (www.dropbox.com), Box (www.box.com), etc., that will store your files locally on your computer and also to "the cloud," so that you'll never be far away from anything you need should something unexpected happen to your computer. Don't forget to keep your fonts and any linked assets (video, audio, etc.) with your presentations so you can easily access them from a different (and hopefully not a new replacement) computer.

## Keep Another Backup of All of Your Files

The Internet is not always where you are. It also has a way of being unavailable or slow at the times when you need it most. Consider investing in a USB drive or a portable external hard drive that can store your presentations and assets, and keep it updated with the latest versions, especially before you travel to a conference.

## Invest in a Really Good Remote

For a while, at least, a number of computers had infrared receivers that were conveniently located on their fronts, in the perfect position for aiming a remote at them from across a room or even across a desk. The funny thing is, they were also conveniently located at the point where the lip of a podium would block the receiver from the remote, rendering the remote fairly useless. This left more than a few presenters baffled about what was wrong, since that remote had worked perfectly well in their home or office.

A good remote isn't cheap. You can expect to spend anywhere from $50 to $100 USD on a remote that can do what you'd like it to do, which, basically, should be controlling your slides from anywhere in a decent-sized room. After a lot of experimentation, we finally asked someone who has given more presentations than the rest of the Internet. Jared Spool introduced us to the Logitech Professional Presenter R800 Remote (www.logitech.com/en-us/product/professional-presenter-r800). As of this writing, it is still a really great remote that works on both Windows and Apple computers. It comes with a green laser pointer and a countdown timer, and it maintains control of your slides from up to 100 feet away.

Determine what features are important to you, ask other presenters what remotes that they use and like—and borrow different ones for trial runs if you can. Then get yourself a nice one that you'll be comfortable with and that has the features you will need.

## Case the Joint

Many organizers may have floor plans or may be willing to take photos of the room that you'll be presenting in so that you can get a general idea of what the room is like. A preview of the space is nice; however, nothing beats physically being in the room to rehearse before you give your presentation.

That said, a lot of events may not offer advance access to the space that you'll be presenting in. You should try to arrive early so you can walk the space, hear how you sound in different areas, and see what other people will see when they're looking at you from their seats. In some cases, you may be fortunate enough to watch someone else presenting in the room, so you can get a sense for what your presentation may sound and look like from the audience.

# Consider the Consequences of That Which You Consume

Have you ever seen that movie *Along Came Polly* where Ben Stiller's character eats at an exotic restaurant and then, suddenly, he breaks into a sweat and his stomach starts gurgling the gurgle that means he's got to...

Yeah.

You want to avoid that.

Be mindful of what you eat and drink prior to getting on stage. Even if you're really comfortable and confident with your material, food and caffeine can have mysterious impacts on your body. Try to avoid anything that can affect your energy level or the way you feel. Some presenters may avoid eating altogether prior to speaking if they know how it can affect them and possibly impact their performance.

**Meet the Expert: Jesse James Garrett, Co-Founder and Chief Creative Officer, Adaptive Path**

Getting ready for a morning talk is really different from an afternoon talk. In the morning, get there early enough that you can get comfortable with the room itself. Have coffee, but do it well before you have to be on stage. I will have something small to eat, not a full breakfast or anything heavy. Don't forget to visit the restroom as close as you can to talk time.

# Watch Other Presentations

If you're at a conference where there is the opportunity for you to see other speakers, before your presentation, you should definitely take advantage of it. Not only do you have the benefit of getting a feel for the energy of the audience, but also you get to hear what other presenters are saying, and you can potentially make references to points that others have made if they relate to your own content.

It may be tempting to hide yourself away and tweak your presentation until it's your turn to get on stage. Do yourself a big favor: Don't do that.

**Meet the Expert: Jesse James Garrett, Co-Founder and Chief Creative Officer, Adaptive Path**

In the afternoon, it's a little different. It's more a matter of watching the other speakers and looking for connections to what you're going to talk about. I don't ever change my presentation—that's too much disruption too late in the game—but I will sometimes add a note referring back to a similar or related point made earlier in the day.

Instead, watch the presentations. Be present. Be respectful to the people who are putting you on the stage, and be part of the community that is their conference. This isn't always easy to do with busy work schedules and family lives, so do what you can to be a part of it all.

> **TIP** You can learn more about different presentation environments in Chapter 5, "Managing the Environment," of the book *Designing the Conversation* by Russ Unger, Brad Nunnally, and Dan Willis.

# Game Time: On the Stage

Once you have your final pre-game preparation out of the way, you're going to want to think about what presenting on stage in front of a real live audience will be like. You'll need to be very self-aware, which can be difficult enough on its own, and you'll also be presenting your material, so you'll be doubly tasked with what you're trying to accomplish. You're essentially patting your head and rubbing your belly at the same time, except you're on a stage and have slides and an audience. You'll want to know what your stage presence is like, how you interact with the onstage environment and elements, and in some cases, how to control the behaviors, patterns, and habits that you might have.

That's right: There's still more to learn and be aware of. No one said this was easy!

It really isn't easy—but it's not super difficult, either. It takes a lot of preparation and practice, and it takes understanding the environments you present in, the tools you present with, and the way that you present.

# Get to Know the Different Types of Microphones

In general, there are three types of microphones that you'll likely encounter as a presenter: the handheld/stand microphone, the lavalier/lapel microphone, and the headset (**Figure 2.3**). The handheld/stand microphone either is stationary or needs to be held while you present, which can be challenging if you're also using a remote to control your slides. By contrast, the lavalier/lapel and headset microphones are hands-free, allowing you to move rather unrestrictedly within a certain broadcast range.

PHOTO BY CAROLE J. BURNS          PHOTO BY DREW MCLELLAN                    PHOTO COURTESY OF BRYAN EISENBERG

**FIGURE 7.3**  The main types of microphones you will encounter: handheld, lavalier/lapel, and headset.

You'll want to understand how to use each of these—the way they operate can be quite different, and how you'll speak when you present can shift slightly depending upon which one you use.

## Handheld/Stand Microphones

The handheld/stand microphone is pretty standard. These are the mics you'll see rock stars belting into while doing stunts with the stands that hold them. At conferences, these are mostly used either with a stand or a clip at a podium, at tables for panels, or for Q&A sessions with the audience.

The important thing for you to learn is how close you should put your mouth to the actual microphone in order to amplify your voice to a reasonable level. Microphones have a funny way of picking up certain sounds, such as Ps, Ts, and Ss in particular, and make them sound, well, kind of awful if you're not careful. There's also no guarantee that each microphone will have the same settings, so you'll want to find out the best position for holding a handheld microphone each time you present.

You can determine the ideal position for holding a microphone through a bit of practice. One way to find the right distance is to start by holding the handle of the microphone with the base at the level of your belly button and a few inches in front of your torso. Then extend out a few inches (adjust for your torso size).

Then practice saying a few words—and *practice* is a great word for you to say so you can understand how those hard *P* and hissy *S* sounds are going to carry. You can try the standard "testing 1, 2, 3" to get a sense of how you sound with the microphone as well. Make adjustments to where you're holding the microphone as you listen to yourself speak, and continue making adjustments while you're speaking as your tone and volume shift. If you want everyone to hear you whispering, hold the microphone close to your mouth, and likewise, move it farther away when you're raising your voice or shouting!

A podium or stand microphone can be treated the same way, except that you'll be moving your head or your body closer to or farther away from the microphone in order to make the adjustments.

It's important to note that not all microphones are created equally, just like all voices do not project with the same force or volume. Practice these techniques so you can get a sense of the best placement of your mouth relative to the microphone. It won't take long, and it'll definitely be worthwhile to get it out of the way early.

> **TIP** You can learn more than you ever wanted to know about microphone techniques by reading the Shure "Microphone Techniques for Live Sound Reinforcement" guide online at http://cdn.shure.com/publication/upload/446/us_pro_mics_for_music_sound_ea.pdf.

### Lavalier/Lapel Microphones

Lavalier/lapel microphones connect via a clip to your shirt or jacket and have a wire that runs to a wireless receiver. These are convenient and comfortable, and by making a few simple up-and-down adjustments while speaking a few test phrases you can find the right placement to get the best sound from them.

One of the most important things to understand with lavalier/lapel microphones is that they work really well as long as you're speaking in the direction in which the microphone picks up sound. Typically, this is straight in front of you, which means that turning your head while speaking is not an option—instead, any turning movement should happen squarely from your shoulders so that you can always be heard through the microphone.

I was once giving a presentation in a very large room with well over a thousand people in it when my copresenter made a comment, and I turned to reply to her. I wasn't aware that the microphone was not picking up my voice, which meant that the audience could only hear her side of our back-and-forth banter, which mostly made me look foolish.

One other thing to note about lavalier/lapel microphones is that the wireless receiver has an on/off switch on it. This allows you to turn them on and off when you cough, sneeze, or do other things, like have side discussions that do not need to be broadcast to the audience. Also, don't be the person who goes to the restroom with her microphone still on.

### Headset Microphones

This microphone will generally hook over your ears and may have wires that surround the back of your head in order to stay secure. It will also likely connect via a cable to a wireless receiver. The microphone rests in front of your face at a position where it will pick up and amplify your audio while you speak naturally. These may take some time getting adjusted to; however, they work quite well and almost are invisible to the audience as you present—and you can turn your head and the microphone moves with you.

## Pay Attention to Your Posture and Other Habits

It's easy to forget to pay attention to your posture and other habits when you're standing in front of an audience. The audience, however, may pick up on the bad habits you have. When you get on stage—and even before, especially when you're in a place where the audience can see you—pay attention to your posture and how you're presenting yourself.

For starters, simply relax. If you're going to be holding a remote, get it ready and have it in your hand, and then let your arms rest at your sides. Stand at relaxed attention—don't slouch, don't cross your arms in front of you or rest your arms at your hips.

The "open position" conveys vulnerability and trust, and it shows others that you're being open, communicating friendliness and positivity. Aim your shoulders at your audience, face your audience, and start your presentation looking at your audience when the time is right. Be natural in your movements and motions—hopefully, you'll have practiced and prepared enough to recognize some of your onstage habits so you'll be very aware of them.

If you're standing behind a podium, take a similar approach and pay extra special attention to where you are looking. It's easy to look at your speaker notes instead of giving your attention to the audience that is in front of you—and don't just look at those in front of you, but pan the room to take in all of the audience, not only the people immediately in your line of sight.

And whatever you do, don't forget to smile! (Unless it's a very serious presentation, and then, by all means, maintain the appropriate somber facial expression.)

## Mind Your Own Stage Quirks

Everyone presents in a different fashion—we all have our quirks and our idiosyncrasies. This is why practice is so important, and why it's especially important to see what you look like on video, if you can. Do you slouch continually? Do you make particular motions before you click on your remote to advance slides? Do you repeatedly say things like "like" and "um" excessively? Do you constantly clear your throat, cough, or sniffle into the microphone?

### Watch Out for Dinosaurs

Get a pen or a pencil.

With your left thumb and your left forefinger, hold one end of the pen or pencil.

With your right thumb and your right forefinger, hold the other end of the pen or pencil.

Hold the pen at your chest level, a couple of inches in front of your chest.

Look at yourself in a mirror.

What do you think you look like? Perhaps a *Tyrannosaurus rex*?

You might as well make a roaring sound now, because you do look like a *Tyrannosaurus rex*.

Presenters may fall into this trap by holding just about anything they've got in this position, which is really easy to do when you have a remote control or a marker in your hands. It's pretty easy to do when you have nothing in your hands as well, and before you know it there's a dinosaur on the stage where a brilliant presenter meant to be.

For more information on the "T-Rex" or other stances and positions that can be distracting, check out *The Exceptional Presenter* by Timothy J. Koegel.

Whatever your quirks are, be aware of them and consciously control them—anything that isn't excessive stands a pretty decent chance of being overlooked by the audience. Anything that distracts from the presentation you're giving should be something that you work to eliminate.

## Be a Real Person, Pinocchio

Be authentic and true to who you are as a person when you're presenting. Don't force your passion onto a topic that you don't really care about, and don't try to invoke a persona that doesn't fit who you are.

In one of my very first presentations, I thought it would be amusing to present in a dry and flat manner. The presentation certainly came across as dry and flat, and I left the stage feeling pretty dry and flat as well. I wasn't conversational, and I wasn't exuding the excitement that I truly had for the topic and for being on stage. Frankly, I'm surprised I was given the opportunity to ever present again, and I learned a lot that day.

Now I really focus on investing a lot of energy and passion into my presentations and giving that back to the audience. I do my best to engage and carry on a conversation; it's what the audience deserves, and it shows them that I'm not the dry droning robot I started out as.

I hope.

## Time Moves Differently When You're on Stage

No, really.

I've got a presentation that has upwards of 80 slides in it, and there have been times that I've given it in 20 to 25 minutes, and others have taken closer to an hour or more. It's the same set of slides, but the audience's engagement, my own excitement and/or anxiety, and the amount of other information that gets worked into—or taken out of—the presentation can vary depending on the day, the type of event, and the types of presentations that I've seen prior to taking the stage.

It's also a lot different when you're up on stage in front of the real audience than it is in front of the mirror. The entire environment is much different; you're probably working with a microphone and a projector, and there are likely a bunch of unfamiliar faces in the audience who are curious to learn from you.

The point is, time has a funny way of shifting once you get on the stage. Remember to speak slowly and enunciate clearly, to take pauses and allow the audience to take notes or send out quips of wisdom to "the Twitters," and to breathe, so as to help keep yourself at the pace you've planned for.

## Don't Let the Audience's Reactions— or Lack Thereof—Deceive You

It's difficult to fully understand the reaction of your audience a lot of times. A joke that was a hit in Albuquerque may totally bomb in Des Moines—or at least seem to. Some audiences may be listening with rapt attention and taking copious notes while you're dropping your wisdom on them, and others may have been forced to attend because their boss couldn't make it and a representative from the team was required to be there. Sometimes, another presenter who hasn't yet taken the stage may make it into your presentation and hunker down in the back to tweak his presentation while you're in the middle of yours. And if you're lucky, you may have one of those *über*talented sketchnoters just trying to keep pace and create a masterful artistic rendition of her notes from your presentation. Regardless of what you're perceiving from the stage, the reality of the audience may be completely different.

Unless your audience is filled with people who are leaning in and nodding at your every word, it can be difficult to understand their reactions. Keep presenting, and try to find someone who is giving genuine reactions to your content. Those people can be your rock and your savior; their feedback can help you understand if—and how—your content is being received.

Some of the best-reviewed presentations have had very quiet audiences, and some of the worst-reviewed have had the crowd in stitches. Learn to keep going and not to let a lack of energy or engagement affect your ability to deliver your content.

## Many Mistakes Aren't All That Obvious

If you've ever seen a live band performance, a live play or musical, or even *Saturday Night Live*, you probably didn't notice very many of the mistakes that were made. That's a pretty great thing to keep in mind, because the same goes for *your* audience, too! In fact, they're likely not going to notice anywhere near as much as you do. When you make a mistake—and you will make mistakes— you'll want to remember the quote "The show must go on," and, of course, keep going on.

### Meet the Expert: Eytan Mirsky, Musician and Actor

Surprisingly—or maybe not surprisingly—most times people are not as aware of any mistakes as you might think. They are not focusing on things the way you (as the performer) are. And even if they do notice some little mistake, they most likely are not going to focus too much on it, especially if they are enjoying the overall performance. Of course, if the whole thing becomes a train wreck, then that's a problem. You just have to keep pushing on. You can also make a joke out of the mistake if that suits your performance style.

If you find yourself in a situation where you've lost your flow, it's completely acceptable to stop, pause, and even let the audience know that you need to restart a part of your presentation, and then continue. Rather than letting this rattle you, do your best to recover—either through taking a moment to get back on track, reviewing your speaker notes (if you have/use them), or simply taking a brief time-out and informing your audience that you want to take a step back and start a section again.

The audience is there for you, and they're happy to do this, because...

## The Audience Wants You to Succeed

Yes, yes. They most certainly do.

The audience is there to see you, and they want to learn from what you've learned. This learning is important to them; they have no real interest or benefit in your failure. They've chosen your presentation, likely from multiple options. They're interested in what you have to say, and they will usually extend you their forgiveness and understanding.

If you keep that in mind when you step on the stage, it can help you give a successful presentation, which is exactly what the audience is looking for!

**Meet the Expert: Susan Weinschenk, Ph.D., Founder, Weinschenk Institute**

One of the toughest things about speaking at a conference is that you often have no idea how many people there will be in the room. If you are one of the "breakout" sessions you could have 4 or 400! I remember one conference I went to speak at—I flew across the country and expected a full room, well, at least 40 people. When it was time for my session, there were four people in the room! I was so disappointed. I could feel myself just wanting to give up, or get through it as fast as possible, or maybe even chuck the whole presentation and just have a conversation with the four people.

But I decided that these four wanted to hear the presentation—that's why they were in the room, and I was going to give it to them. Four or 40 or 400, it didn't matter! So I gave the best presentation I knew how to give. The four people really appreciated it, and I even ended up landing one of them as a client. It's always nice to have a full room, but don't let it stop you if you don't.

Plan your presentations so that they will work with 4 or 400, and then give the best presentation you can every time.

# The More You Do It, the Easier It Gets

There are so many things to be aware of and to pay attention to when you're presenting that it can be daunting to consider them all. If you give yourself enough time for planning, preparation, and practice, the hardest part will be taken care of—knowing your content to the extent that you can comfortably talk about it. From there, it will still take some time to acclimate to the infinite variety of venues that you may present in.

Find opportunities to give your presentations in front of different groups and at different venues so you can continue to learn and become comfortable with yourself on the stage. Before you know it, you'll start to establish your own routines that will allow you to give your best presentations with less stress and mental overhead.

# 8 MANAGING THE AUDIENCE

Most of the important things in the world have been accomplished by people who have kept on trying when there seemed to be no hope at all.

—Dale Carnegie

A lot of things will come to mind when you think about the audience for your presentation. The most important thing to remember is that the audience is, in general, your friend. They *want* you to succeed before you even set foot on stage—they've read that brilliantly crafted abstract that you uncovered in your brainstorming and supported with a bio that has explained exactly why you are on the stage, and they are in their seats. Still, there are things *you* can do when preparing and when presenting that can help the audience help you give a great presentation.

# Pre-Gaming

Do your homework. Ask your conference chairs about the audience you can expect—what their demographics are, how much experience they have, where they are coming from, what their backgrounds are—and how your presentation will fit into the overall theme of the conference. The more you know, the better you can be prepared to give your best presentation for the audience in front of you.

While we're mostly going to focus on working with audiences from the stage, there are some things regarding your audience that you can consider and manage prior to starting your presentation.

## How Will You Hand Out Materials?

Sometimes you may want or need to provide materials—this could be handouts, pens or pencils, product samples, etc.—to your audience. When planning, do your best to determine the maximum number of people you may have in your audience so that you can have enough for everyone. In fact, if you can make this a digital component, you should do so, to avoid having entirely too few or too many copies for everyone.

Sometimes, however, you won't have the digital luxury. Talk to the people who manage the conference, and ask them if you can find out how many people will be attending overall and how many you might expect in your particular session. This is important to clarify—some conferences have multiple rooms or tracks running simultaneously, and it's safe to say that not all of the attendees will choose your session, so it's good to ask for some input. If all else fails, take the total number of attendees, divide by the number of simultaneous sessions, and then add about 25 percent more on top of that in order to be safe.

Next, you'll want to determine the best time to share those materials with your audience. Do you want to arrive early and have those items on the seats waiting for people to arrive—or will that be a distraction from the content you'll be presenting? Will you have an assistant or someone in the room with you who can help you distribute your materials when they're needed? Plan ahead, and identify the best approach for sharing items with your audience in a minimally distracting and optimally efficient manner, so it won't throw off the timing of your presentation.

## Where Do You Want the Audience?

Audiences can be very tricky, and they can have minds of their own when it comes to choosing where they'll sit within the room that you're presenting in. If you've got a room that seats 50 people and you have 30 to 50 in it, you'll be okay; however, if you're in a room that easily holds 1,200 and you've only got about 70 to 80 in it (<cough>personal experience<cough>), well, things can get a little challenging.

### Pro Tip: Moving Your Audience

A speaker at the WebVisions conference in Portland, Oregon, was presenting in a very large room and had an attendance that was substantially less than the room's maximum capacity. Mind you, this wasn't due to the presenter's popularity; it was simply a room that was better suited for handling closer to a thousand people rather than tens or hundreds of people.

People had been scattering throughout the large room during presentations on the previous day, and it was clear that some presenters had struggled to interact with the audience. This wise presenter came up with a solution that was not only a bit humorous, but also very effective. He purchased a few dozen Voodoo Doughnuts, placed them at the front of the stage, and offered them to anyone who was willing to come sit up front, which of course, was where he felt he could better present to them.

For the low cost of the doughnuts, the bribe worked in the presenter's favor, and he was able to form a better connection with his audience.

Given the opportunity, audiences will spread out a bit and will not always sit close to the stage where you can easily see or, perhaps, interact with them. It's kind of like being in a movie theater—people will do their best to put space between their group and other groups, unless the movie is wildly popular, and then everyone sits elbow to elbow.

Remember that you've got the microphone and some authority. You can either spend an entire presentation wishing that the audience was closer to you, or you can spend 30 seconds feeling slightly uncomfortable and ask them all to move closer. You may lose a couple of people if you do that, or some simply may not play along, and that's okay—they probably weren't the attendees you were hoping for. Once your audience is in a better position, you'll feel much more at ease giving your presentation.

# Getting to Know the People in the Audience

In general, we know that the audience, as a whole, wants you to succeed. That audience is a melting pot of all different types of people and personalities who are all unique in their own special ways. But despite that uniqueness, there are some patterns and groups—for example, energy givers and energy takers—that these people fit into, and you can learn a few ways in which to work with them.

## Energy Givers

When you're presenting—and you're hopefully comfortable enough and familiar enough with your material that you're looking out into your audience—there are certain types of people that are awesome to see. These are the people who can give you a boost or a lift as you're presenting, because they're giving you feedback that lets you know that the message in your content is being received in a positive way.

I like to call these people the "energy givers" because that's exactly what they do—they give you positive energy by letting you know that they're digging what you're sharing. You'll notice them because they're listening in rapt attention, leaning forward and taking in every word you're saying. Sometimes, they're nodding along with the things you're saying, seeming to tell you that they've been through what you're presenting about, and they're happy that they've found someone else who's had a similar experience.

While you can assume that everyone in the audience typically wants you to succeed, the energy givers are going to flat out let you know, and you should take note of them. Lean on them when you feel like you're struggling in your presentation; their reactions and responses can give you the extra boost of assurance you need to keep your confidence high.

# Energy Takers

Sometimes, you may find a person who appears to react as if he or she does not agree with you or the points you're making during your presentation. Even worse, you may imagine a negative vibe coming from an audience member. This can suck the energy right out of you and can take your focus away from the material that you are presenting, turning it instead toward the way that you are feeling. When you start to feel as if there's an energy taker in your audience, look for those energy givers and lean on them if you need to. It's unlikely that anyone in your audience will stand up and disrupt your presentation while you're in the middle of it, so continue to focus on your content and get yourself back on track.

You may also notice people in your audience who are potentially disruptive. These may be people carrying on a whispered, yet audible, conversation or the people who arrive late or leave early (and, even worse, close the door noisily). These may be people who appear to be disinterested or focused on other things that have nothing to do with your presentation. There are really any number of things that might be slightly unsettling from your view on the stage.

Some people may want to "help" you—or, more specifically, they know a lot about your subject and want to be a part of the presentation. It is likely that they do this not out of malice, but rather out of a desire to be helpful; however, that doesn't make it any less of a break in your flow and a shift in your energy. Sometimes, they may be polite enough to raise their hands while you're speaking, and if you call on them, they may choose to expound more on their own information, or even different information, than what you've provided. You need to remember that you're the person on the stage for a reason, and you can politely ask them to wait until the end of your presentation so as to respect the time slot that you're working within. You don't have to feel obligated to take questions during your presentation; that is up to you.

It's rare, but you may encounter someone who interrupts you to dispute a point that you're making or to attempt to heckle you in some way. This can be really disconcerting and can knock even the most seasoned professional for a loop. It's pretty disrespectful, and audiences don't appreciate someone disrupting the presentation and making them feel uncomfortable. Without matching the disrespect, you can ask the person to wait until the end of your presentation so that you can address his interruption then, or you can ask to speak to him later. Hopefully, he will accept this response; if he doesn't, you may need to enlist the support of the conference chairs to help you resolve the issue.

## Meet the Expert: Jared Spool, Founder, UIE

I was presenting at a meeting of about 150 people in the East Bay of San Francisco. I was giving a presentation that I'd given several times already, and I was comfortable with the content. It was a description of facets of what made Web 2.0 interesting, and the talk had multiple sections, where I explored each facet.

Normally, I'd just move through the entire presentation and take questions at the end. As I was finishing up the first section, an audience member put his hand up and wouldn't take it down. I tried to ignore it, but eventually I recognized him and let him present his question.

Instead of asking a question, he started to explain something I'd already presented, in more detail and from his own perspective. He was mostly right, but not completely, and I didn't want to correct him in front of the audience, so I thanked him and resumed my presentation.

As I finished the next segment, up came the same person's hand with more helpful advice. I could tell that the rest of the audience wasn't excited to hear his expansion; plus, he was now extending my presentation, which was already quite packed for the time allotted.

When he raised his hand the third time, I said, "It's clear you know a ton about this stuff. I recommend that people find you after the presentation to get all this helpful, additional information. In the meantime, because we need to get home, I'm going to finish my presentation for now, okay?"

After that, the audience gave a fairly visible sigh, and he contained himself for the rest of the presentation.

**NOTE** As the presenter, you have authority and control on your side, and you can establish some rules of engagement for your audience. You can also choose how you react when someone breaks those rules, and you can do that with the help of your microphone, which enables you to be louder than just about any negative person in the audience.

The flagrant disrupters are few and far between. Don't spend a lot of time and energy being anxious about a pretty uncommon edge case; just remember to be as respectful to those who are disrupting as you wish they were being to you. If you're concerned that your topic might be controversial enough to warrant extra support, discuss this with your conference chairs long before ever taking the stage.

## The Unknowns

In addition to the energy givers and energy takers, there are those audience members whom you just may not know how to interpret or engage. These include those factions of people who are sitting out in the rows of chairs and looking down—perhaps at a laptop, phone, or phablet/tablet—doing who knows what. They might be tweeting something #awesome you just said or something that was featured on one of your slides. They might be sketchnoting and creating something really cool that they can show their friends and family after your presentation, or they simply might be ignoring your presentation altogether and getting some work done while they're filling a seat. All of these things are okay—and they happen regularly at conferences. These people make it difficult to understand their motivation for being in the room, and the trick here is not to worry about it. Let these people do what they're doing and focus on the energy givers as much as you can.

There are some other people who fit into this "unknown" category. You may have friends, family, coworkers (or—Heaven forbid—your boss), other speakers, or even conference chairs sitting in on your talk. Sometimes, people who chair other conferences might be sitting in the audience and scouting you to see if you'd be a fit for an event they're planning. These can all be either good or bad additions to your audience, depending on how these types of people affect your stress level.

Do your best to give your best presentation; over time, you'll learn to sharpen your focus and just give your presentation without worrying about who is in the audience. Until that point, remember that the audience wants you to succeed, and it's very likely that these "unknowns" are there to support you. Let them support you, and turn that support into positive energy.

# Q&A

Inevitably, when presenting, you will end up in a situation where your audience will have questions. While you don't have to allow for Q&A, you'll also likely not cover all of the aspects of your topic that are important to everyone in the audience, and it's good to share your knowledge beyond the presentation. As you learn what people are curious to know more about, it will help you further refine your presentation in the future.

We've gathered some basics of Q&A that can help you as you get started in your presentation career.

## Repeat the Question

You're likely the only person in the room with a microphone, so unless there is a volunteer or conference staff member taking a microphone to people who are asking you questions, you'll want to repeat the question the audience member is asking. If nothing else, you should repeat the question to confirm that you heard it right, especially if the person asking took a long approach to getting to the question. This can help you make sure you're answering correctly, and it helps the audience fully hear the question and your response.

## It's OK to IDK

If you don't know the answer to someone's question, that's absolutely fine. Simply state that you don't know and ask if you can follow up with the person asking the question.

It's impossible for you to fully know every aspect of any topic you present, unless your topic is the creation of the lathe, and you were the actual creator of the lathe. Even then, it's possible that you hadn't considered everyone else's use cases for the lathe, so it would be okay not to know the answer to every lathe question, too.

It's always better to let your audience know that you don't know than it is to try to BS your way to an answer that just fills up time. Be straight with your audience and move things along, and you'll be fine.

## It's OK to Be Wrong

This might be tough to believe, but it's okay if you make a mistake. If someone points out a mistake that you made in your presentation, and you can recognize that you made a mistake, then acknowledge the mistake, apologize for the mistake, promise to correct the mistake, thank the person asking the question, and move on. Owning a mistake will earn you more points than any back-and-forth battle of words ever will—unless you're not wrong, and then you need to find a polite way to explain your case.

## Manage the Question Asker

Sometimes, an audience member may have her own anecdote, a long statement that isn't actually a question, or a confusing way of getting to the question that she's asking you. You can play the "Repeat the Question" game if you can get her to the point of the question. Be aware of the time and the other people in the audience who may also have questions. If it's taking too long, ask your question asker to talk to you offline, after the presentation Q&A is over. Be mindful of how you handle this situation; the majority of questions are not ill intended.

Sometimes people relate to the presentation you've just given, and they're happy to have found someone who shares an interest or an experience that is similar to theirs. As you've been learning, there's a lot that goes into putting together a presentation; asking a relatively unprepared question can sometimes be pretty difficult for the question asker (who suddenly has an opportunity to talk to you and realizes that a room full of eyes are now on her). Have a little empathy, try to coach the person asking the question, and if it's starting to take up too much time, promise a conversation when the Q&A is done—and follow through with that.

## Get Out of the Way

Unless you're the last person presenting before lunch or at the end of the day, pay attention to how much time is left before the next presenter. Be aware of how long you can stick around in your room and handle Q&A, too—not only might there be other presenters who have to set up after your talk, but your conference hosts may have a time limit set upon them, meaning that people have to exit the space by a certain time or additional fees may be incurred.

Once you start your Q&A, pay attention to how much time is left for your session. Make sure you stick to the amount of time that you're allotted, and if it's at all possible, start the teardown of your equipment so that you can get out of the next presenter's way—so long as it doesn't detract from the attention you need to give the audience while handling Q&A. In some cases, the conference may have staff who are ready to help you with that; let them do their job while you do yours.

> **TIP** You can learn more details about Q&A in Chapter 18, "Managing Q&A," of the book *Designing the Conversation* by Russ Unger, Brad Nunnally, and Dan Willis.

# Tricksy Humanses

Audiences are unknown, uncontrollable factors of your presentation. They can influence the amount of energy and excitement that exists in the room during your presentation. A joke that went over perfectly with an audience in Tucson might bomb in Des Moines. You'll want to learn to read audiences, and make adjustments to your own style, pace, and even your content so you can give each your best possible presentation.

Get comfortable with yourself on stage and then get comfortable with reading audiences and interacting with them, and you will give yourself more chances for success. Most importantly, you should remember that the audience is there for you, and they want you to succeed.

# 9 ITERATING YOUR PRESENTATION

The improvement of understanding is
for two ends: first, our own increase of
knowledge; secondly, to enable us to
deliver that knowledge to others.

—John Locke

Whew.

You've finally done it. You've managed to go from having a spark of an idea all the way to presenting live on a stage at a conference! This is pretty exciting and heady stuff, and if things went well, you'll likely be trying to figure out what your next big idea should be...

Are you ready to do it all over again?

Don't be so quick to rush out and start seeking more new ideas for presentations. Instead, take a moment and just sit right there and think about other conferences or events that might be a good fit for the presentation you just gave. Unless the presentation was very specifically focused for the conference and only had relevance to the audience you just presented to, there's a good chance that you can find another audience who would enjoy and benefit from your presentation.

Before you start reaching out to line up your next speaking gigs, take some time and examine your performance of the presentation you just gave. Oh, and don't do this just once—do this each time you give the presentation. You'll undoubtedly find areas of the presentation you can tweak or revamp to make it even better the next time you present it.

# Room for Improvement

There are some key areas of your presentation that you should pay attention to and consider making adjustments to. Don't go easy on yourself, and at the same time, don't beat yourself up so much that you throw the baby out with the bathwater. If you're having some difficulty deciding where to make updates, go back to the outlining phase and look for ways to shift your content before you go messing with your full presentation.

In some cases, conference chairs will collect feedback on the sessions and provide that directly to the presenters. Take advantage of this gift and make sure that you thoroughly review all comments. This may require a bit of intestinal fortitude. Not everyone is going to be well versed in the fine art of critique, and some feedback can be downright harsh, yet even in the harshest criticism you may find nuggets of insight that you can use for improvement.

**NOTE** Before you do anything to your presentation, make sure you save a backup copy before you start making any major changes. This allows you not to permanently destroy content that you may have use for at a later date or in a different presentation.

## The Title and Abstract

Now that you've given your presentation live in front of a real audience, do your title and your description still feel as if they're accurate and appropriate for the content? Think back to the information that you shared with your audience as you review your title and description with fresh eyes. Make updates to ensure that everything syncs together nicely, makes sense, and provides conference chairs and reviewers with a clear expectation of what you'll be presenting on.

## Your Slides

As you presented, did you notice how your slides worked with your content? Review your slides to make sure that all of your in-slide transitions and slide-to-slide transitions are accurate and correct, and timed accordingly. It seems that the first couple of times I give any presentation, there is always a transition error that I don't catch until the rehearsal. Now's the time to fix those mistakes if they slipped through into the live show.

Next, consider whether your fonts, styles, and copy were correct and readable on your slides. Work through the presentation and fix any contrast issues between the copy and the background that you may have overlooked until you saw it projected on a different screen than on your own computer and make any stylistic adjustments that might be needed. Don't forget to go back through your presentation to correct any typos you may have noticed, too.

Revisit your original outline and compare it to the content that you're currently working with to make sure that you've identified the right flow for anything that you're adding in or removing. You may need to review all of your content to make sure that any new themes permeate all of the presentation content that you have so that it feels natural and connected throughout.

### Meet the Expert: Karen McGrane, Managing Partner, Bond Art + Science

I think the biggest difference between good speakers and truly great speakers is the great ones give each talk multiple times. Less-experienced speakers sometimes think they must write a new talk for every event. But giving a talk over and over is how you polish the delivery. It's not wrong to give a talk you've given before—in fact, it's respectful of your audience to put the work into getting it right. And even as an audience member, I don't mind hearing the same talk from a speaker more than once, because I always get something new out of it.

I might add new slides or change the order of them when the talk is very new, but after I've given a talk a few times I'm happy with the flow. After that, I focus on delivery. Certain lines will get a laugh, so I work on getting the timing right. Sometimes I'm explaining a complex concept, and I want to be precise in how I express it. After I've given a particular talk around 20 times, I'd say about half of it is memorized—I deliver those lines exactly the same way every time I do it. I have some talks I've given 40 times or more, and I don't ever get bored with them. When I know the content of a talk really well, that's when I have the luxury of being able to perfect the delivery.

## Timing, Pacing, and Flow

We've already mentioned that "stage time" passes a lot differently than rehearsal time, so you'll want to see how well your content presented against the amount of time that you were allotted. If you went over, did you have too much content, or were there any distractions or activities that took longer than you anticipated and caused you to come up short on time?

In the event that your presentation fell far short of your time (even while trying to allow for 5 to 10 minutes of Q&A), did you speak really quickly and fly through your material without taking enough time to breathe or to let the audience keep up with you? Or did you find yourself going over your allotted time or finishing really close to the end? Perhaps there are sections of your content that you should reduce or cut out entirely—or maybe you're trying to cram two different presentations into too broad of a topic. Don't be shy when it comes to removing content, and, if anything, cut mercilessly while continuing to make revisions.

If you feel that the flow between your topics wasn't very smooth (and you'll definitely know when this happens), look for opportunities to improve the content so that your topics connect in a logical, sensible way. Sometimes this can be as simple as identifying numbered steps or points that your audience can learn from, and sometimes you may need to weave in a good story with strong connections to make the connections happen in a way that doesn't feel too forced.

Also, pay extra special attention to any questions you got from the audience—these can uncover key opportunities to expand or refine your content in order to improve your presentation. As you're making updates, review your content and your outline again to make sure that you're staying within the focus of your original topic.

## Closer to Fine

After you've reviewed and revised your content based upon what you've learned from presenting live to an audience, well, you're still not done. It's time to take a step back and practice the presentation again with your revisions in place. You'll want to make sure that all of the changes you made are making sense and fit into the flow of your content. Any time you make adjustments to your presentation, you'll want to familiarize yourself with the way the updated content works so that you'll be prepared the next time you present.

You might even want to review Chapter 6 all over again.

# Again and Again and Again

You should treat each time that you give your presentation live in front of an audience as practice for the next time you give the presentation. It's also practice for any future presentations that you give, as you'll start to understand how different factors affect your performance—from the drinks and food you consume (or don't) to your slot in the schedule, to the person you present before or after, to the room and audience size, to... so many other factors.

Don't invest all of this time and effort into giving a presentation just once—continue to improve it and update it until the time comes that you decide to sunset it. This could be months or even years, depending on how relevant your topic is and how many audiences find it valuable

As long as you're focused on continually improving for your next audience, it will show in your presentations. It's hard work doing this presentation stuff, no matter how easy and effortless it may appear to be from the seats in the audience. Some people are genuinely gifted and can make their time on the stage seem really natural to them—most of us, however, have to work our tails off to fool audiences into thinking that.

Invest the time and strive to get better and you will get better, and your audience will appreciate you for it.

# Additional Resources

We've gathered some of our favorite resources to help you learn more about becoming a better presenter:

- *The Exceptional Presenter* by Timothy J. Koegel
- *The Confident Speaker* by Harrison Monarth and Larina Kase
- *Presentation Zen* by Garr Reynolds
- *So What?* by Mark Magnacca
- *Designing the Conversation* by Russ Unger, Brad Nunnally, and Dan Willis
- *The Naked Presenter* by Garr Reynolds
- *Slide:ology* by Nancy Duarte
- *Confessions of a Public Speaker* by Scott Berkun
- *100 Things Every Presenter Needs to Know About People* by Susan Weinschenk
- *The Non-Designer's Presentation Book* by Robin Williams
- *Presentation Zen Design* by Garr Reynolds
- *Resonate* by Nancy Duarte

# Index

Unlimited online access to all Peachpit, Adob
Press, Apple Training, and New Riders videos
and books, as well as content from other
leading publishers including: O'Reilly Media,
Focal Press, Sams, Que, Total Training, John
Wiley & Sons, Course Technology PTR, Class
on Demand, VTC, and more.

No time commitment or contract require
Sign up for one month or a year.
All for $19.99 a month

## SIGN UP TODAY
**peachpit.com/creativeedge**

**creative**
edge